French - Greek

LEARNING FLASHCARDS

FOR BABIES TODDLERS

alligator

αλλιγάτορας

The alligator is having a party.

fourmi

μυρμήγκι

The ant is red.

ours

αρκούδα

The bear loves you.

abeille

μέλισσα

The bee is saying hello.

oiseau

πουλί

The bird is flying.

papillon

πεταλούδα

The butterfly is pretty.

chameau

κάμηλα

The camel has a hump.

chat

γάτα

The cat is happy.

dinosaure

δεινόσαυρος

The dinosaur is laying eggs.

poulet

κοτόπουλο

The chicken is dancing.

vache

αγελάδα

The cow has a bell.

cerf

ελάφι

The reindeer has a toy.

chien

σκύλος

The dog has two floppy ears.

dauphin

δελφίνι

The dolphin is swimming.

canard

πάπια

The duck has a bow.

aigle

αετός

The eagle is looking for food.

l'éléphant

ελέφαντας

The elephant is sitting.

poisson

ψάρι

The fish is a clownfish.

libellule

λιβελούλα

The dragonfly is blue.

renard

αλεπού

The fox has a red nose.

grenouille

βάτραχος

The frog is smiling.

girafe

καμηλοπάρδαλη

The giraffe has a long neck.

chèvre

γίδα

The goat has a beard

ver de terre

σκουλήκι

The worm is in the apple

poule

κότα

The hen has chicks.

hippopotame

ιπποπόταμος

The hippo is big.

cheval

άλογο

The horse is fast.

kangourou

καγκουρώ

The kangaroo has a baby.

chaton

γατάκι

The kitten is playing.

lion

λιοντάρι

The lion has a mane.

homard

αστακός

The lobster is red.

singe

πίθηκος

The monkey has a tail.

poulpe

χταπόδι

The octopus has food.

hibou

κουκουβάγια

The owls have big eyes.

panda

αρκτοειδές ζώο της ασίας

The panda wears a diaper.

porc

χοίρος

The pig is fat and pink.

chiot

κουτάβι

The dog is brown.

lapin

κουνέλι

The rabbit has a carrot.

rat

αρουραίος

The mouse is writing something.

crabe

κάβουρας

The crab has two pinchers.

requin

καρχαρίας

The shark is scary.

mouton

πρόβατο

The sheep are very fluffy.

escargot

σαλιγκάρι

The snail is slow.

serpent

φίδι

The snake has poison.

araignée

αράχνη

The spider is purple.

écureuil

σκίουρος

The squirrel has a nut.

tigre

τίγρη

The tiger has a red bow.

tortue

χελώνα

The turtle has a shell.

loup

λύκος

The wolf is smiling.

zèbre

ζέβρα

The zebra is black and white.

dinde

τουρκία

The turkey has two legs.

coq

πετεινός

The rooster will crow.

perroquet

παπαγάλος

The parrot is colorful.

hérisson

σκατζόχοιρος

The hedgehog has apples.

pomme

μήλο

The apple has a leaf.

abricot

βερύκοκκο

The apricot is yellow.

avocat

αβοκάντο

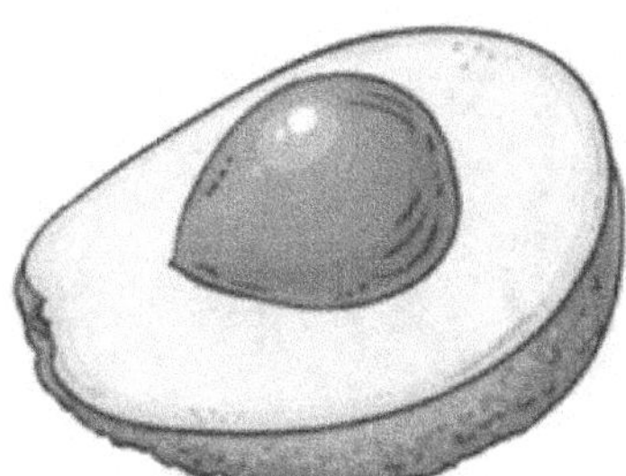

The avocado has a nut.

banane

μπανάνα

The banana is yellow.

la mûre

μαυρο μουρο

There are a lot of blackberries.

cassis

είδος φραγκοστάφυλλου

The blackcurrants are yummy.

myrtille

μυρτιλός

The blueberries are sweet.

cerise

κεράσι

The cherries have a stem.

noix de coco

καρύδα

The coconuts have juice.

figues

σύκα

The fig has seeds.

grain de raisin

σταφύλι

The grapes are purple.

pamplemousse

φράπα

The grapefruits are sour.

kiwi

ακτινίδια

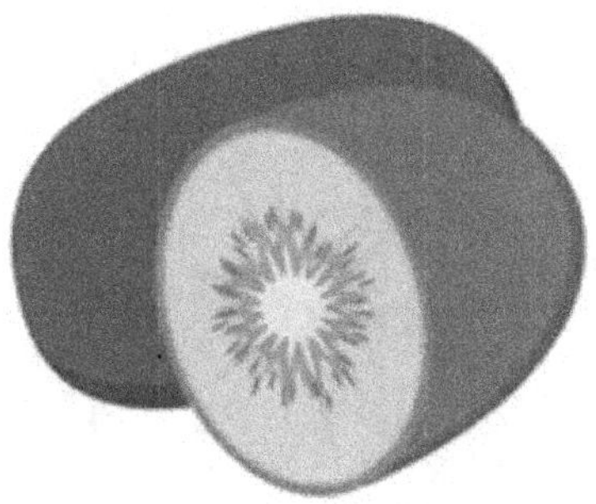

The kiwi is fresh.

citron

λεμόνι

The lemons are yellow.

citron vert

άσβεστος

We have lots of lime.

litchi

λυκείο

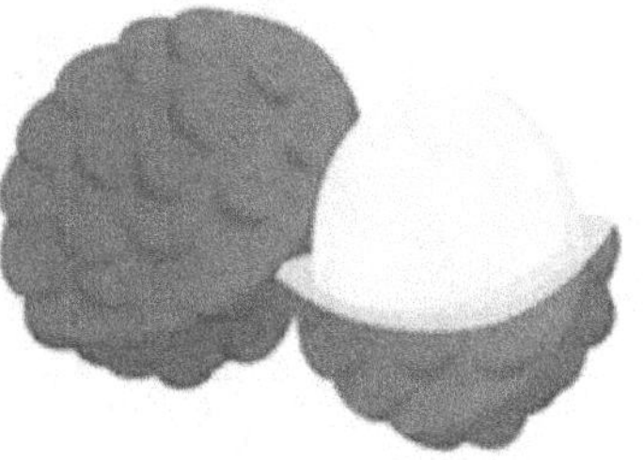

I like to eat lychee.

mandarine

μανταρίνι πορτοκάλι

Oranges are refreshing.

mangue

μάνγκο

Mango is my favorite fruit.

orange

πορτοκάλι

Mandarins are like oranges.

papaye

παπάγια

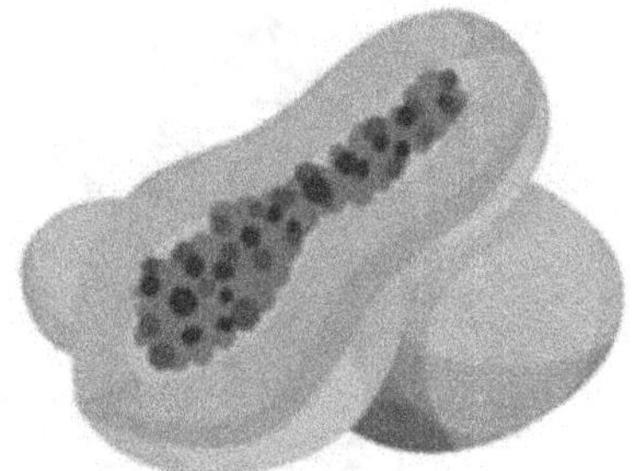

Papayas have lots of seeds.

pêche

ροδάκινο

Peaches are juicy.

poire

αχλάδι

Pears have a strange figure.

ananas

ανανάς

The pineapple has a thumbs up.

prune

δαμάσκηνο

Plums are healthy for you.

grenade

ρόδι

Pomegranates are all red.

framboise

βατόμουρο

The raspberry is shiny.

fraise

φράουλα

The strawberry has leaves on top.

pastèque

καρπούζι

The watermelon is big.

mandarine

μανταρίνι

The tangerine looks like an orange.

tarte

πίτα

I like to eat apple pie.

gâteau

κέικ

That cake is huge.

bonbons

καραμέλα

Candy is not good for your teeth.

biscuit

κουλουράκι

Cookies are easy to make.

donut

ντόνατ

I like strawberry donuts.

crème glacée

παγωτό

The ice cream is melting.

muffin

τηγανίτα

The muffin has a cute wrapper.

pudding

πουτίγκα

We eat pudding on Christmas.

classeur

βιβλιοδέτης

I keep pictures in my binder.

livre

βιβλίο

I like to eat books.

sac à dos

σακιδιο πλατης

The backpack has lots of stuff.

les ciseaux

ψαλίδια

I have scissors in my bag.

épingles

καρφίτσες

Pins can hold stuff up.

agrafe

συνδετήρας

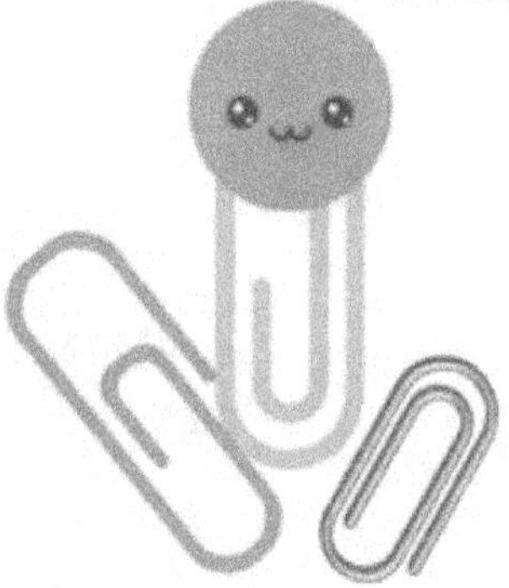

Clips can hold up paper.

papier

χαρτί

I have lots of paper.

agrafeuse

συρραπτικο

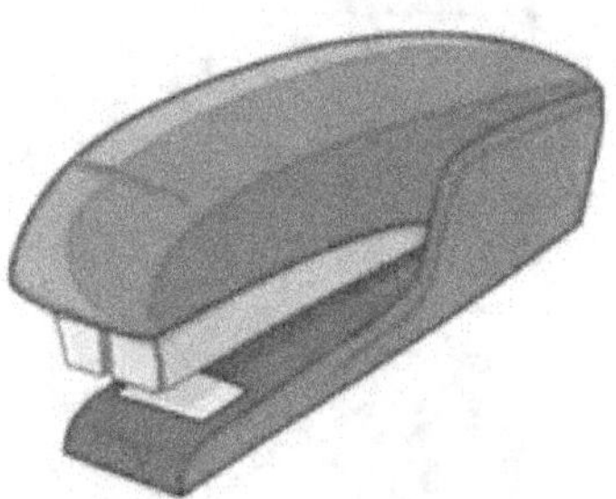

My stapler is shiny and red.

calculatrice

αριθμομηχανή

My calculator has buttons.

règle

κυβερνήτης

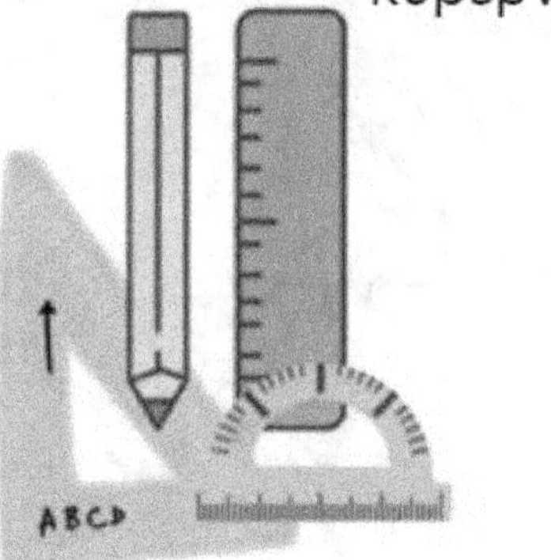

I have lots of rulers.

la colle

κόλλα

The glue is sticky.

bibliothèque

βιβλιοθήκη

My bookcase has lots of things.

calendrier

ημερολόγιο

I have a calendar on my table.

chaise

καρέκλα

My chair is fancy.

l'horloge

ρολόι

The clock says that it's 3 o'clock.

ordinateur

υπολογιστή

I do things on my computer.

bureaux

γραφεία

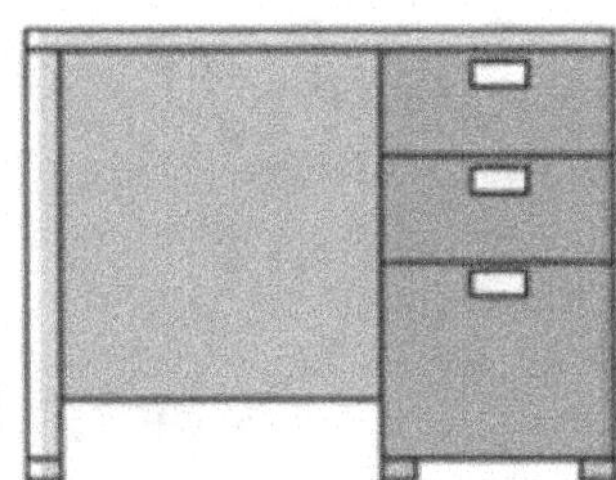

I put lots of things on my desk.

dictionnaire

λεξικό

The dictionary has lots of words.

la gomme

γόμα

Erasers are used with pencils.

carte

χάρτης

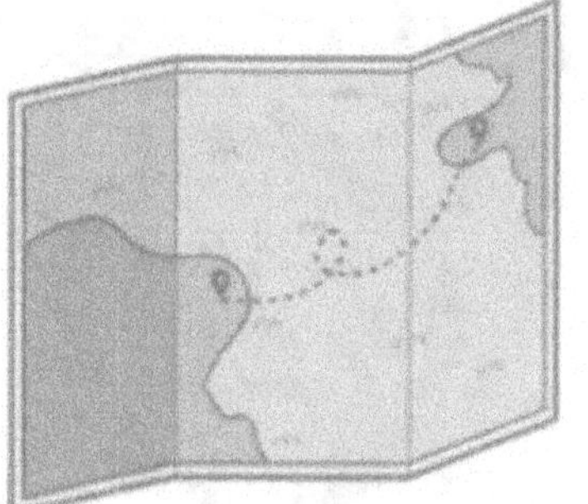

The map shows you different places.

carnet

σημειωματάριο

I use notebooks at school.

stylo

στυλό

My pen is very pretty.

crayon

μολύβι

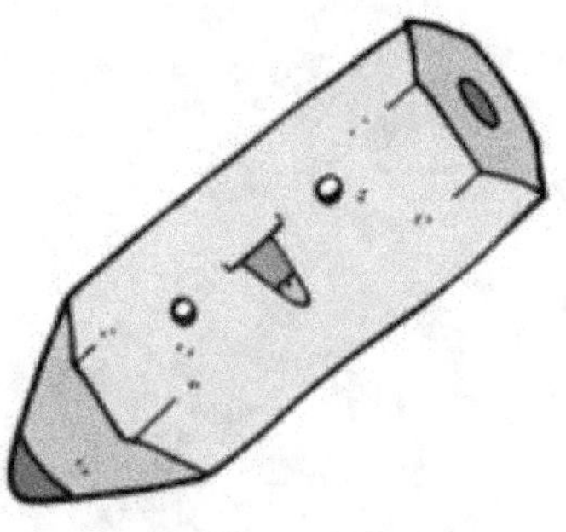

My friend gave me a pencil.

ceinture

ζώνη

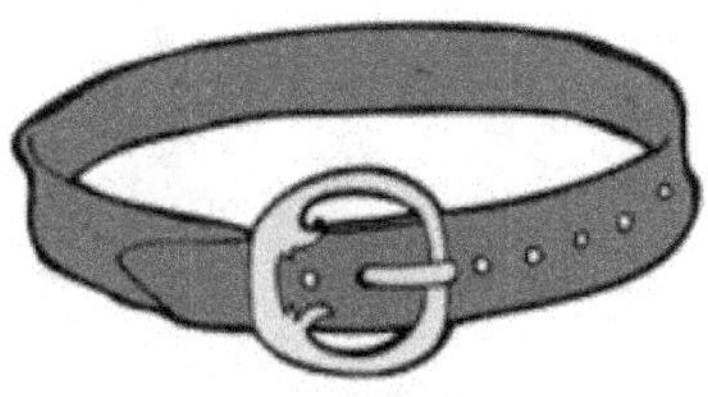

I have a belt on my pants.

bottes

μπότες

I have big brown boots.

chapeau

καπέλο

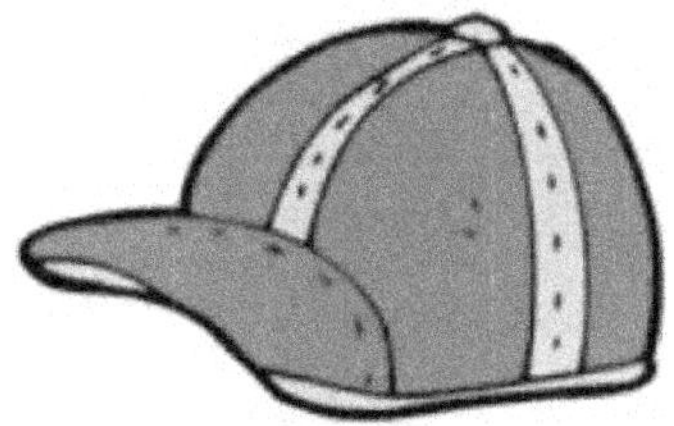

My mom bought me a new cap.

manteau

παλτό

She has a long yellow coat.

robes

φορέματα

My dress has a bow.

gants

γάντια

I got new gloves.

chapeau

καπέλο

That hat is for a wicked witch.

veste

σακάκι

The jacket is cozy.

jeans

τζιν παντελόνι

My jeans are long.

pyjamas

πιζάμες

I sleep in my pajamas.

un pantalon

παντελόνι

The bear is wearing pants.

imperméable

αδιάβροχο

We wear our raincoats when it is raining.

écharpe

κασκόλ

The baby has a scarf around his neck.

chemise

πουκάμισο

I like this shirt the best.

des chaussures

παπούτσια

I have red and blue shoes.

jupe

φούστα

My skirt has lots of buttons.

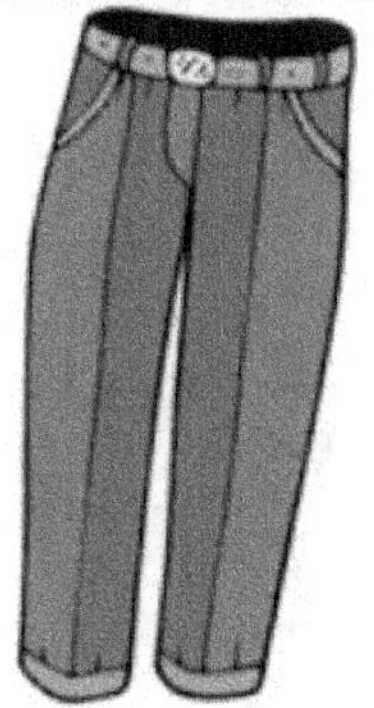

pantalon

πλατύ παντελόνι ανάπαυσης

My dad wears slacks.

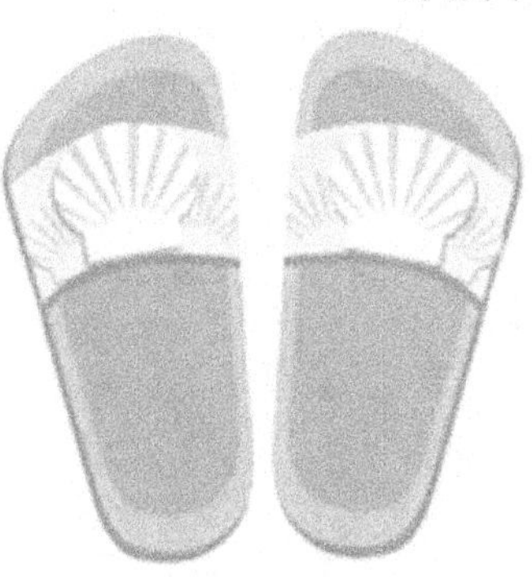

chaussons

παντούφλες

I have seashells on my sandals.

chaussettes

κάλτσες

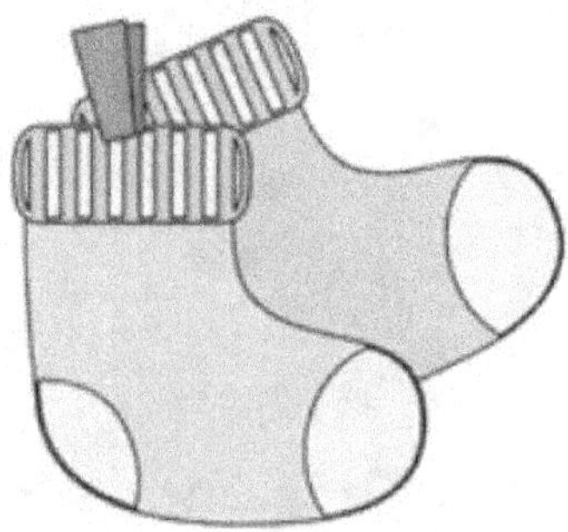

My baby sister wears socks.

costume

κοστούμι

My brother is wearing a suit.

chandail

πουλόβερ

I am wearing a sweater for winter.

cravate

γραβάτα

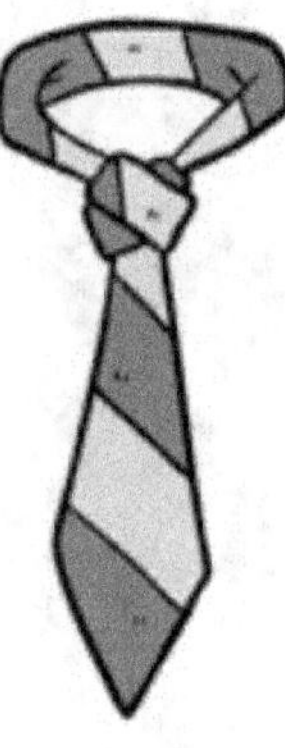

My dad wears a tie to meetings.

pantalon

παντελόνι

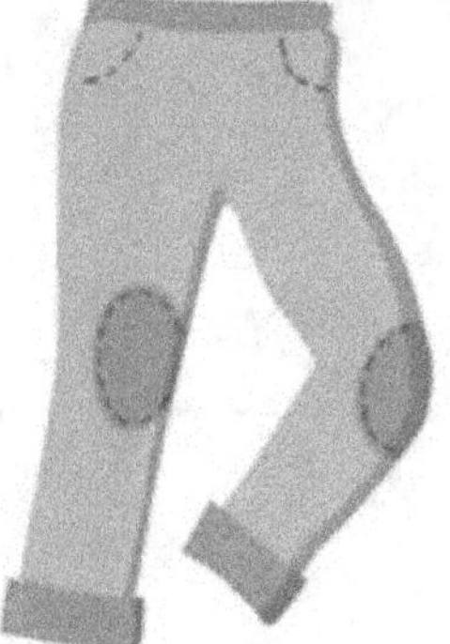

The trousers look like jeans.

slip

σώβρακο

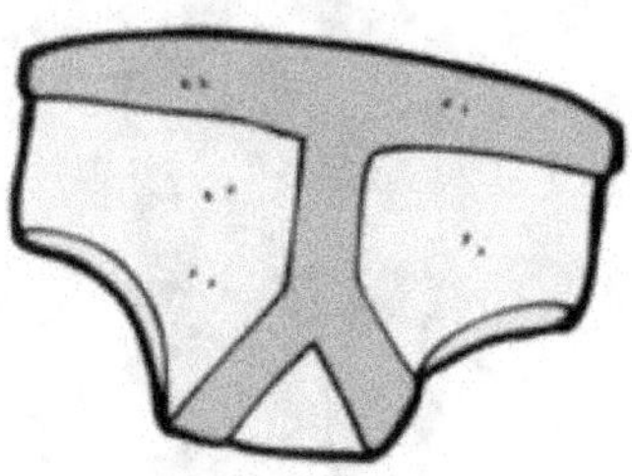

I always wear my underwear.

maillot de corps

εσώρουχο

My undershirt has a star.

une

ένας

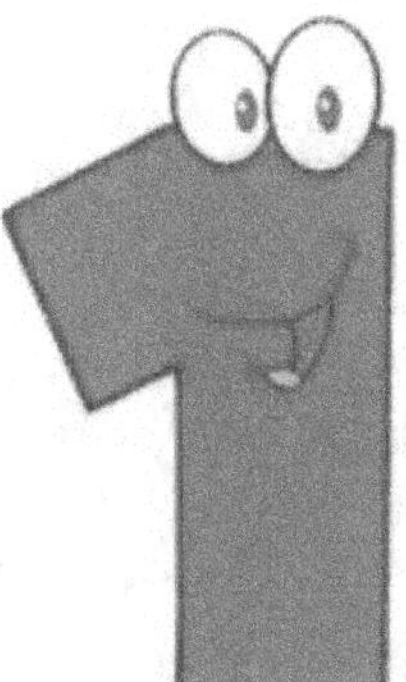

Number one and the bee are friends.

deux

δύο

The cat and the mouse both love two.

trois

τρία

The bear gives number three a present.

quatre

τέσσερα

Number four is a home for the cat.

cinq

πέντε

Number five hatches an egg.

six

έξι

Number six is going to eat a carrot.

sept

επτά

Number seven is playing with the tiger.

huit

οκτώ

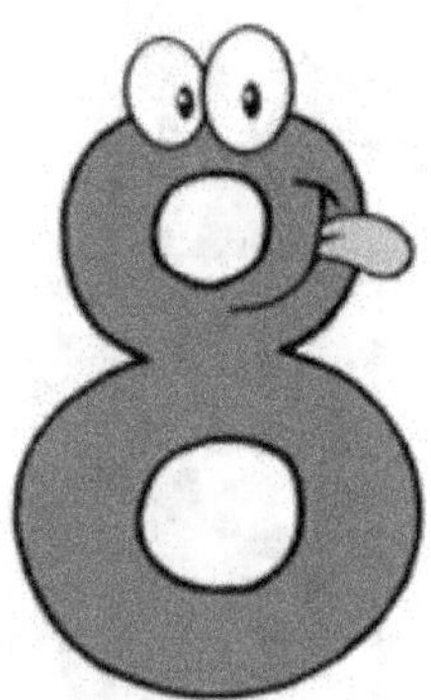

Number eight is funny.

neuf

εννέα

Number nine meets the parrot.

dix

δέκα

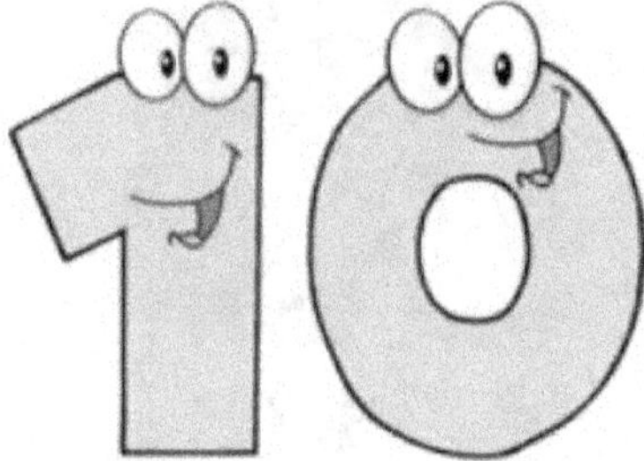

Number ten is smiling.

onze

έντεκα

Number eleven has big eyes.

douze

δώδεκα

Number twelve is number one and two.

treize

δεκατρείς

Number thirteen is excited.

quatorze

δεκατέσσερα

The number fourteen is vast.

quinze

δεκαπέντε

The number fifteen is green.

seize

δεκαέξι

Sixteen is my lucky number.

dix-sept

δεκαεπτά

Number seventeen look alike.

dix-huit

δεκαοχτώ

Number eighteen will go to the circus.

dix-neuf

δεκαεννέα

I am nineteen now!

vingt

είκοσι

Number twenty has a zero.

fourmi

μυρμήγκι

The ant has lots of legs.

cloche

κουδούνι

The bell will ring.

vache

αγελάδα

The cow has a bow.

poupée

κούκλα

She has a cute bear doll.

oeuf

αυγό

The chick has hatched out of the egg.

poisson

ψάρι

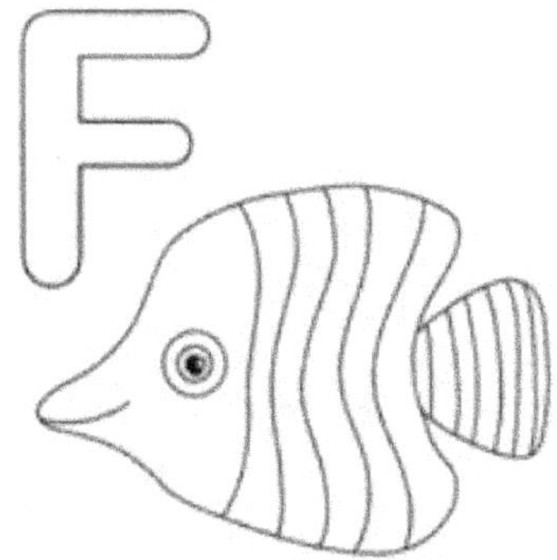

The fish is swimming in the water.

chèvre

γίδα

The goat is sitting on the grass.

chapeau

καπέλο

He is wearing a hat.

crème glacée

παγωτό

I like to eat ice cream.

confiture

μαρμελάδα

The kitten is sitting on the jam jar.

chaton

γατάκι

The cat is sleeping on the floor.

lion

λιοντάρι

The lion is waiting for the tiger.

rat

αρουραίος

The mouse has lots of presents.

nez

μύτη

The reindeer has a red nose.

hibou

κουκουβάγια

The owl is sleeping.

porc

χοίρος

The pig will eat cupcakes.

reine

βασίλισσα

The queen has a big crown.

lapin

κουνέλι

The rabbit is jumping up and down.

mouton

πρόβατο

The sheep have fluffy wool.

tortue

χελώνα

The turtle has a shell.

parapluie

ομπρέλα

The mouse is holding an umbrella.

van

βαν

The van is driving along the road.

pastèque

καρπούζι

The watermelon has lots of seeds.

xylophone

ξυλόφωνο

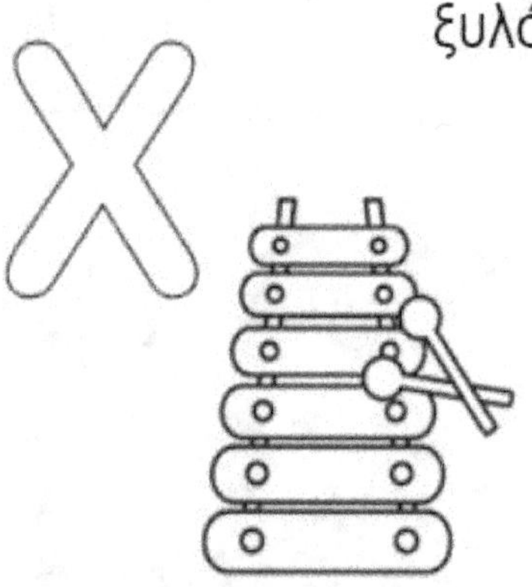

We are going to play the xylophone.

yaourt

γιαούρτι

We opened the yogurt can.

zèbre

ζέβρα

The zebra is surprised.

rose

ροζ

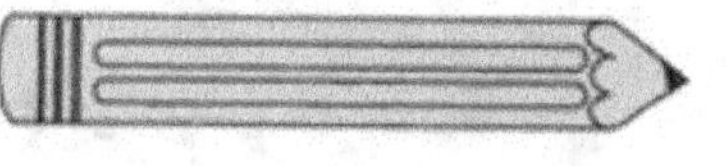

color the word and
the picture in pink

Most of my clothes are pink.

marron

καφέ

color the word and
the picture in pink

brown

My chocolate is brown.

gris

γκρί

color the word and
the picture in pink

gray

I don't like the color gray.

vert

πράσινος

color the word and
the picture in pink

green

The vegetables are green.

jaune

κίτρινος

color the word and
the picture in pink

yellow

Bananas are yellow.

blanc

άσπρο

color the word and
the picture in pink

white

The paper that I write on is white.

rouge

το κόκκινο

color the word and
the picture in pink

red

Apples are red.

bleu

μπλε

color the word and
the picture in pink

The night sky is blue.

percer

τρυπάνι

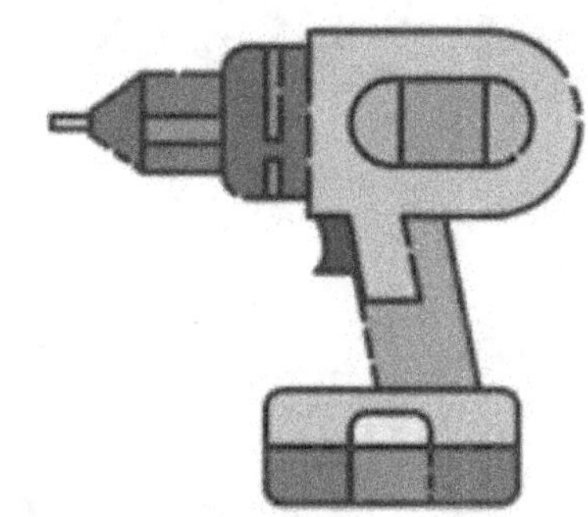

The drill will help us fix this.

marteau

σφυρί

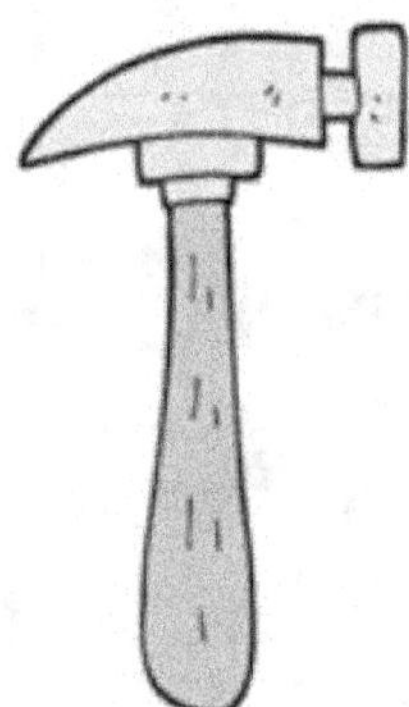

The hammer is going to nail the picture.

couteau

μαχαίρι

The knife is sharp.

pinces

πένσα

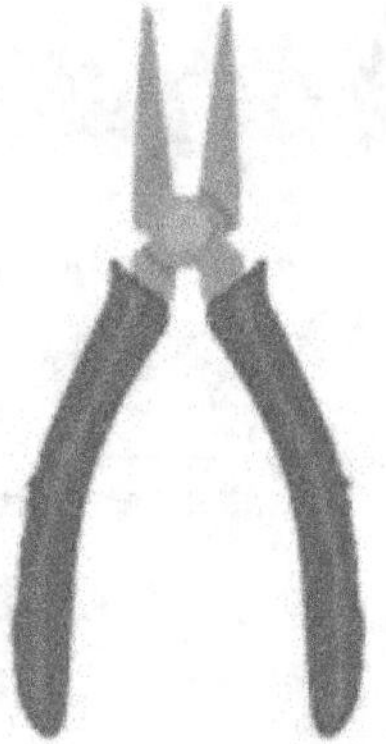

The plier is used for many things.

vu

πριόνι

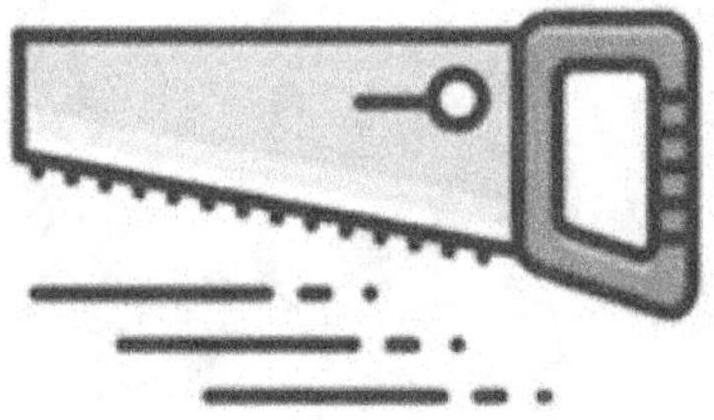

The saw can chop wood.

les ciseaux

ψαλίδια

I use scissors to cut paper.

tournevis

κατσαβίδι

The screwdriver can screw in the knots.

clé

γαλλικο κλειδι

The wrench can help unscrew the knots.

avion

αεροπλάνο

The airplane is going to leave now.

vélo

ποδήλατο

The bicycle is beautiful.

bateau

σκάφος

The boat is floating on the water.

autobus

λεωφορείο

The bus is going to school.

voiture

αυτοκίνητο

The car is green.

hélicoptère

ελικόπτερο

The helicopter is looking for something.

cheval

άλογο

You can ride the horse.

jet

πίδακας

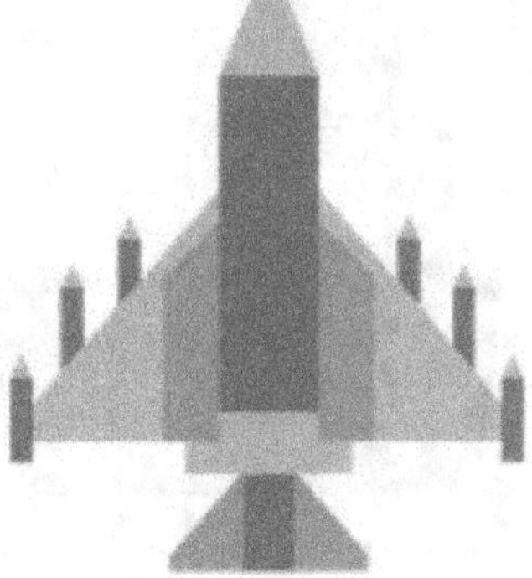

The jet is high-speed.

moto

μοτοσυκλέτα

The motorcycle is on the road.

navire

πλοίο

The ship is on the water.

métro

μετρό

My mom goes on the subway to work.

taxi

ταξί

The taxi has someone inside.

train

τρένο

The train is going slowly.

un camion

φορτηγό

The truck has stuff in it.

asperges

σπαράγγι

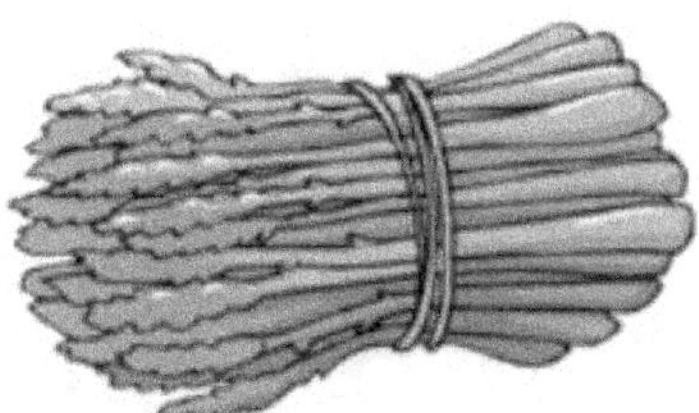

The asparagus is in a bundle.

des haricots

φασόλια

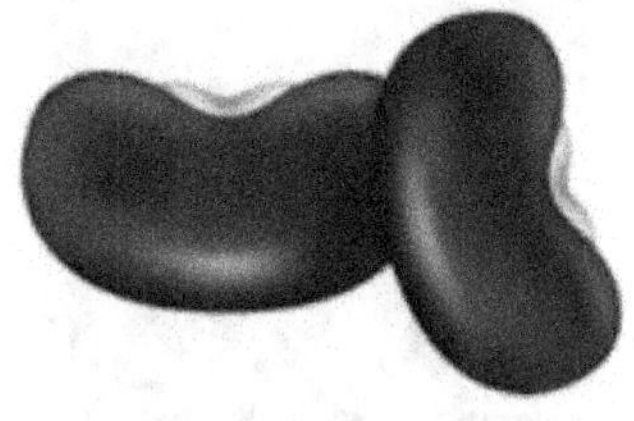

The beans are smooth.

brocoli

μπρόκολο

The broccoli is dancing.

chou

λάχανο

Bunnies like to eat cabbage.

carotte

καρότο

The carrots are very long.

céleri

σέλινο

The celery has lots of leaves.

blé

καλαμπόκι

Corn soup is delicious.

concombre

αγγούρι

The cucumbers are cut into pieces.

aubergine

μελιτζάνα

The eggplant is purple.

poivre vert

πράσινο πιπέρι

The green pepper is juicy.

salade

μαρούλι

The lettuce is all green.

oignon

κρεμμύδι

The onions make my eyes water.

pois

αρακάς

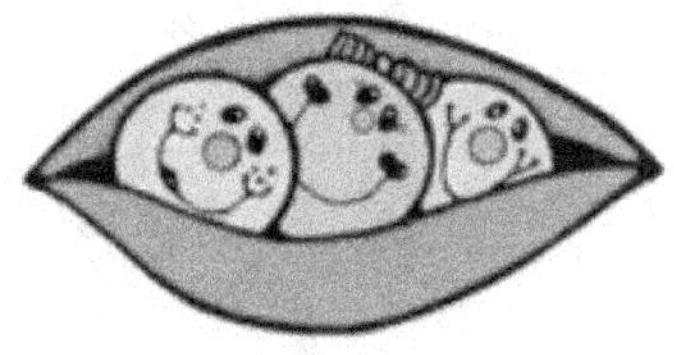

The peas are all in a pod.

patate

πατάτα

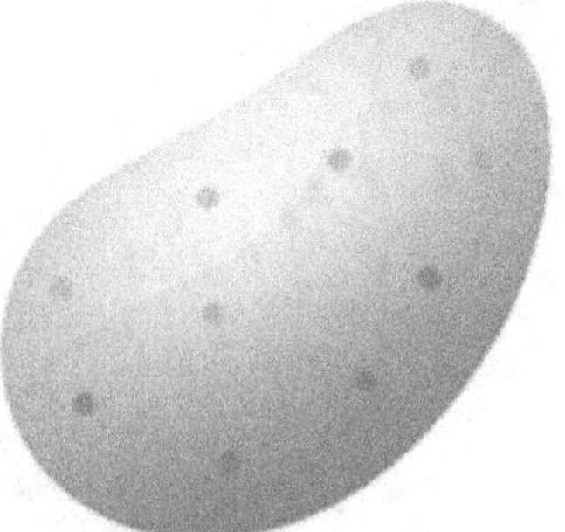

The potato is very shiny.

citrouille

κολοκύθι

The pumpkin is for Halloween.

un radis

ραπανάκι

The radish is a type of vegetable.

épinard

σπανάκι

The spinach is good with cheese.

patate douce

γλυκοπατάτα

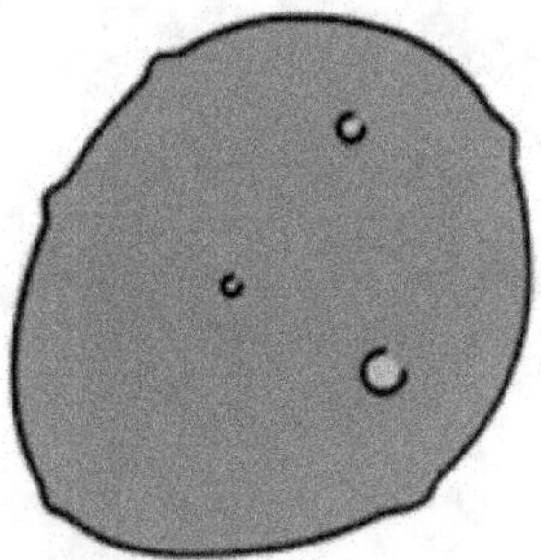

The sweet potato is quite sweet.

tomate

ντομάτα

I don't like to eat tomatoes.

navet

γογγύλι

My mom bought some turnips.

nuageux

συννεφιασμένος

The weather is cloudy today.

du froid

κρύο

I like cold weather.

cool

δροσερός

The temperature is cold today.

brumeux

ομιχλώδης

The fog is so strong I can't see the city.

chaud

ζεστό

The fire is burning hot.

humide

υγρός

It's so humid and wet today.

pluvieux

βροχερός

It's raining very hard.

neigeux

χιονώδης

Welcome to snow land!

orageux

θυελλώδης

I hate the stormy weather.

ensoleillé

ηλιόλουστος

The sun is shining!

chaud

ζεστός

The whole world is warm today!

venteux

ανεμώδης

The leaves are blowing away since it's so windy!

tante

θεία

My aunt is very nice to me.

frère

αδελφός

My brother is very fun to play with.

cousin

ξαδερφος ξαδερφη

I love going to the playground with my cousin.

fille

κόρη

I like to read books with my daughter.

père

πατέρας

My father is playing with me.

petite fille

εγγονή

My granddaughter has blond hair.

grand-mère

γιαγιά

My grandmother is very old and has glasses.

petit fils

εγγονός

My grandson and I are very excited today!

mère

μητέρα

My mother likes to pick me up.

neveu

ανιψιός

My father's nephew is my cousin.

nièce

ανηψιά

My niece is very good at playing ball.

sœur

αδελφή

My sister is so pretty!

fils

υιός

My son likes to play with toy cars.

belle fille

προγονή

My stepdaughter likes the color orange.

belle-mère

μητριά

My stepmother is pretty.

beau-fils

παραγυιός

This is my stepson, Greg.

oncle

θείος

My uncle tells lots of funny jokes.

bol

μπολ

The bowl has nothing inside.

tasse

φλιτζάνι

My mom drinks her coffee out of a cup.

plat

πιάτο

That dish has a bone inside.

fourchette

πιρούνι

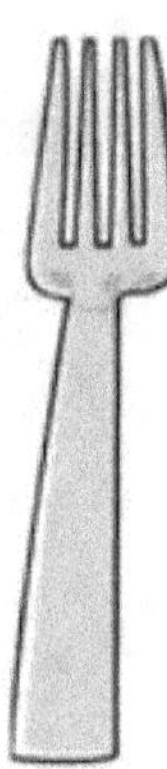

We have more spoons than forks.

verre

ποτήρι

I have a glass of water on my desk.

couteau

μαχαίρι

I have a knife in my kitchen.

agresser

κούπα

This mug of coffee is for my dad.

serviette de table

χαρτοπετσέτα

You can use the napkins to clean your hands.

poivre

πιπέρι

The pepper is very spicy.

lanceur

στάμνα

Pour yourself some lemonade from the pitcher.

assiette

πλάκα

Can you help me wash the plates?

salade

σαλάτα

The salad is very healthy for you.

sel

άλας

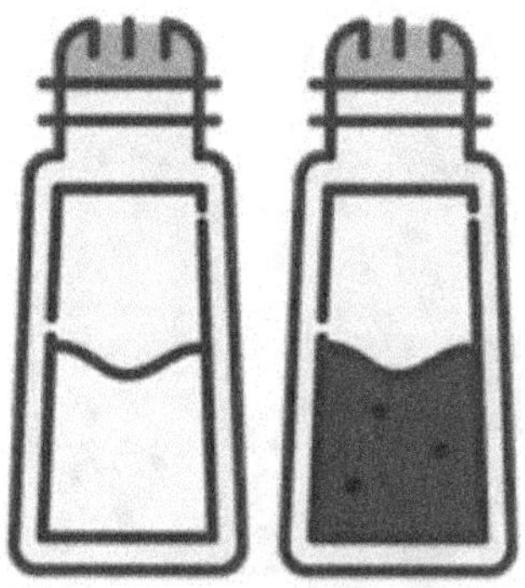

The salt tastes good with a few pinches of pepper.

soucoupe

πιατάκι

The plate is for my cup.

cuillère

κουτάλι

I use a spoon to eat my rice.

sucre

ζάχαρη

The pack of sugar is very heavy.

dimanche

κυριακή

Sunday

Sunday is the day to go to Church!

lundi

δευτέρα

Monday

Monday is the day to start school.

mardi

τρίτη

Tuesday

We will go to the shops on Tuesday.

mercredi

τετάρτη

Wednesday

Wednesday is hard to spell!

jeudi

πέμπτη

Thursday

Thursday is the fourth day of the week!

vendredi

παρασκευή

Friday

My birthday is on Friday!

samedi

σάββατο

Saturday

Saturday is the weekend!

cuire

ψήνω

The chef will bake a cake.

ébullition

βρασμός

I will boil the eggs.

griller

ψήνω στη σχάρα

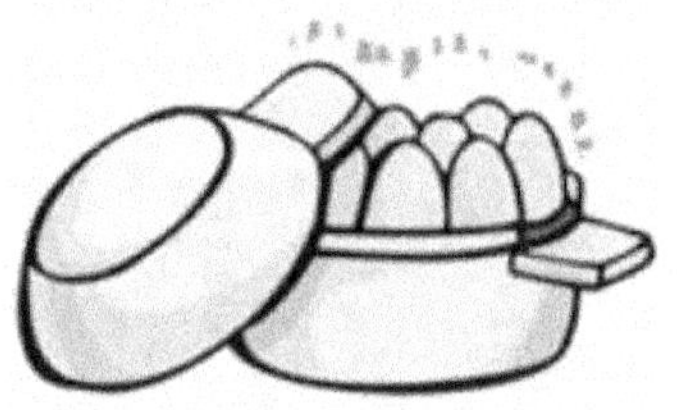

Broil is very yummy.

ouvre-boîte

ανοιχτήρι

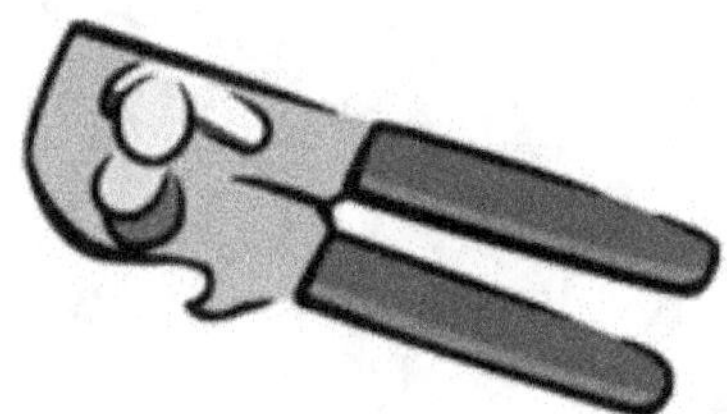

That can opener is used for
opening cans.

frire

μαρίδα

The pan can fry lots of things.

gril

ψηνω στα καρβουνα

We have a grill in our backyard.

tasse à mesurer

κύπελλο μέτρησης

My mom uses the measuring cup
for baking.

cuillère à mesurer

κουτάλι μέτρησης

I use a measuring spoon to eat my dessert.

four micro onde

φουρνος μικροκυματων

The microwave is used to heat food.

bol à mélanger

μπολ ανάμιξης

She is using the mixing bowl to mix things.

serviettes en papier

χαρτοπετσέτες

Dry your hands with paper towels.

poché aux œufs

λαθραίο αυγό

The poach is put on noodles.

porte pot

κάτοχος δοχείου

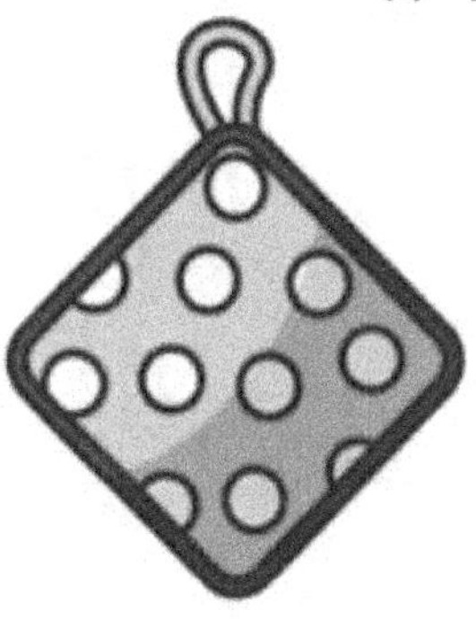

The potholder is soft.

rôti

ψητό

The chef made roast chicken.

rouleau à pâtisserie

πλάστης

He is holding a rolling pin.

brouiller

σκαρφάλωμα

My mom is making scrambled
eggs for breakfast.

mijoter

σιγοβράζω

The simmer is rice today.

couteau

μαχαίρι

The knife is sharp.

cuillère

κουτάλι

I eat my food with a spoon and
fork.

spatule

σπαθί

The spatula will help us flip the steak over.

vapeur

ατμός

The steam is coming from the pot.

passoire

σουρωτήρι

The strainer is used to strain stuff.

minuteur

μετρών την ώραν

I set my timer for 12:00.

fourchette

πιρούνι

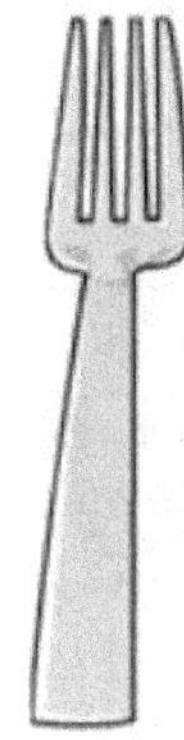

I have lots of metallic forks.

grille-pain

φρυγανιέρα

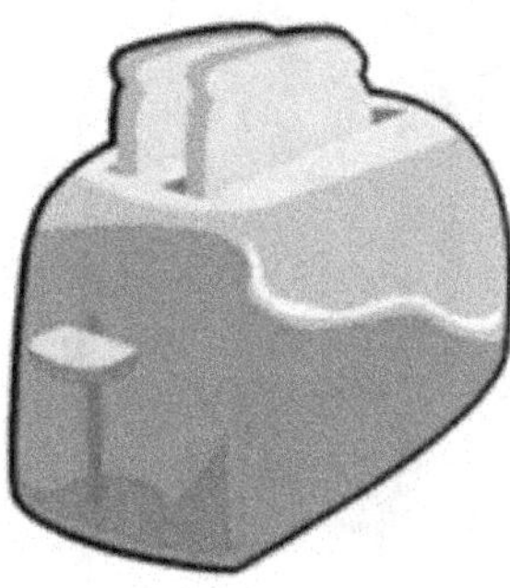

The toaster will toast my bread.

bouilloire

βραστήρας

The kettle has tea inside.

réfrigérateur

ψυγείο

The refrigerator has lots of things inside.

mixeur

μίξερ

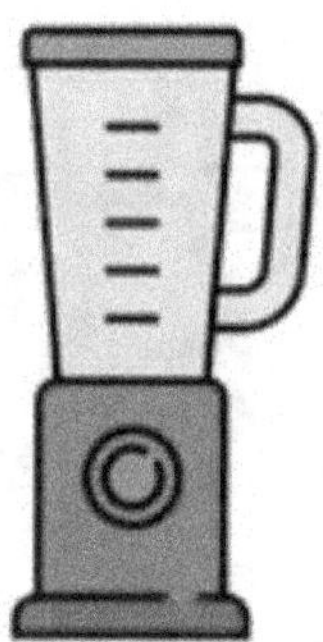

The blender will mix up my fruits.

cabinets

ντουλάπια

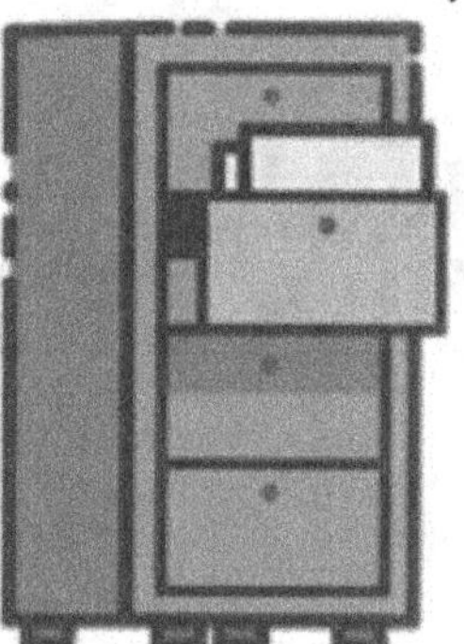

The cabinet has my paper inside.

placard

ντουλάπι

The cupboard has lots of books.

four micro onde

φουρνος μικροκυματων

The microwave will heat my food.

arrière

πίσω

She has a slender back.

des joues

μάγουλα

She kisses her mom on the cheek.

poitrine

στήθος

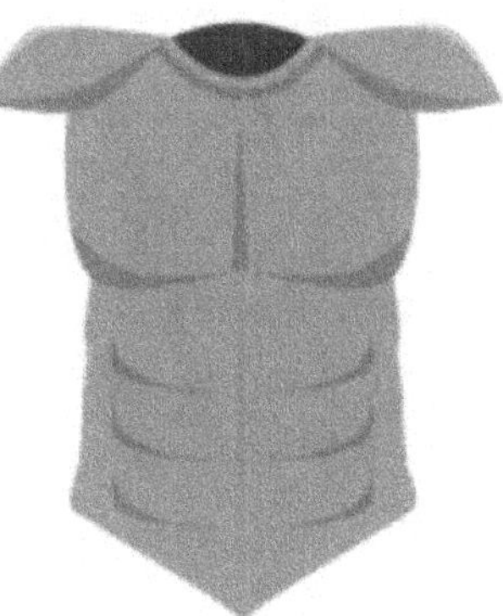

The armor is for your chest.

menton

πηγούνι

This is my chin!

oreilles

αυτιά

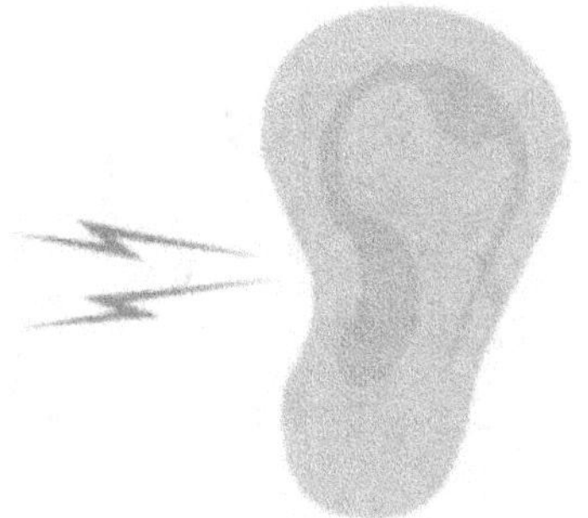

The ear is hearing something.

les sourcils

φρύδια

The eyebrows are raised.

yeux

μάτια

The eyes are blue.

pieds

πόδια

I have one pair of feet.

des doigts

δάχτυλα

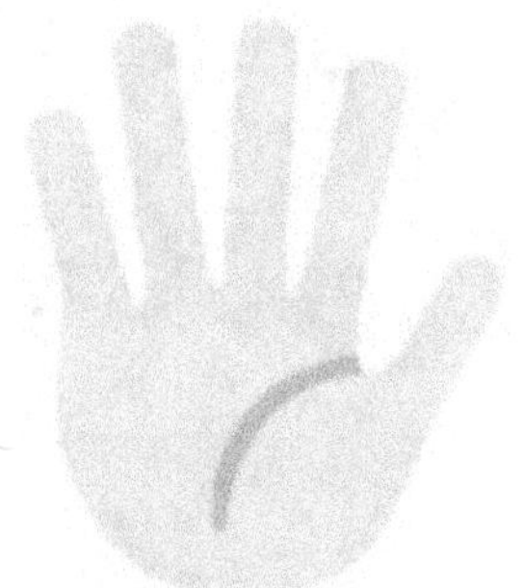

The fingers are waving at us.

pied

πόδι

My foot has five fingers.

front

μέτωπο

My brain is behind my forehead.

cheveux

μαλλιά

My hair is long and black.

mains

τα χέρια

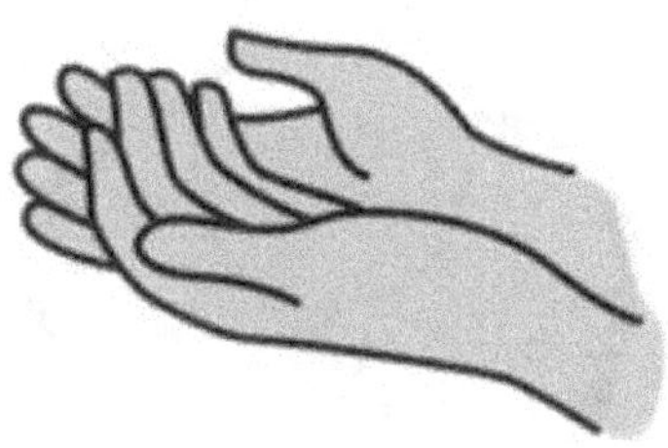

I will wash my hands in the sink.

tête

κεφάλι

She has a big head.

les hanches

γοφούς

The gorilla has his hands on his hips.

les genoux

γόνατα

She is begging on her knees.

jambes

πόδια

The tiger has strong legs.

lèvres

χείλια

The lips have lipstick on.

bouche

στόμα

He is covering his mouth with his hand.

cou

λαιμός

The necklace is very special to me.

nez

μύτη

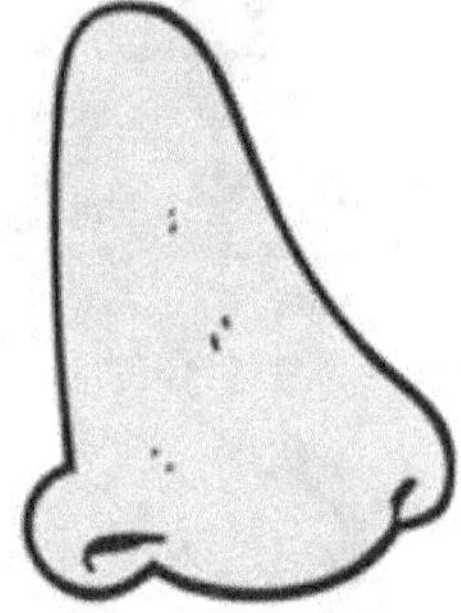

The nose smells something.

épaules

ώμους

He puts his hands on his shoulders.

estomac

στομάχι

He has a big stomach.

les dents

δόντια

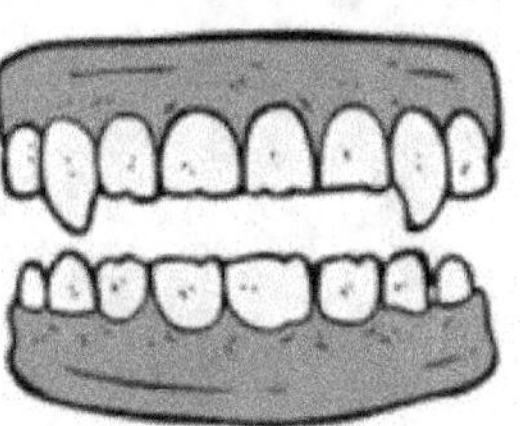

The teeth are clean and white.

gorge

λαιμός

He has a sore throat today.

les orteils

δάχτυλα των ποδιών

My toes are small.

langue

γλώσσα

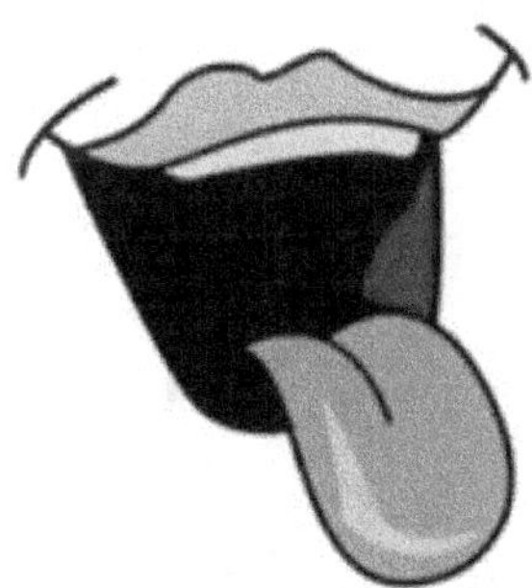

My tongue is licking ice cream.

dent

δόντι

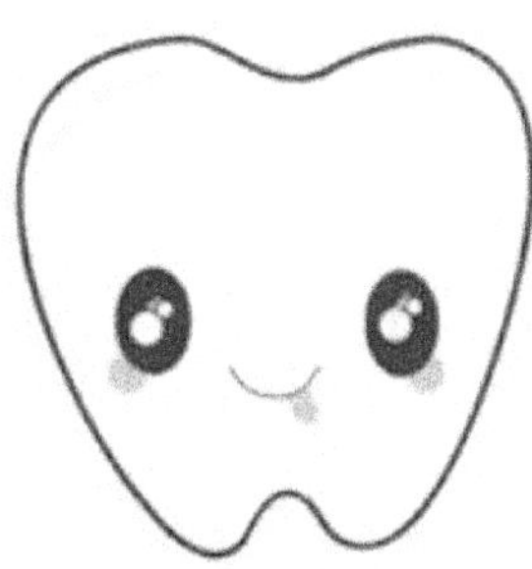

The tooth has big eyes.

taille

μέση

He has his hands on his waist.

salopette

φόρμα

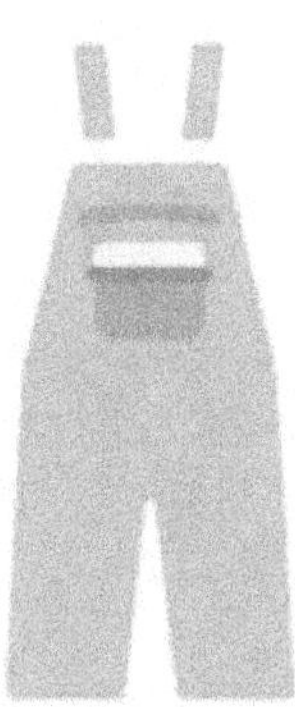

I bought these overalls for you!

mitaines

γάντια

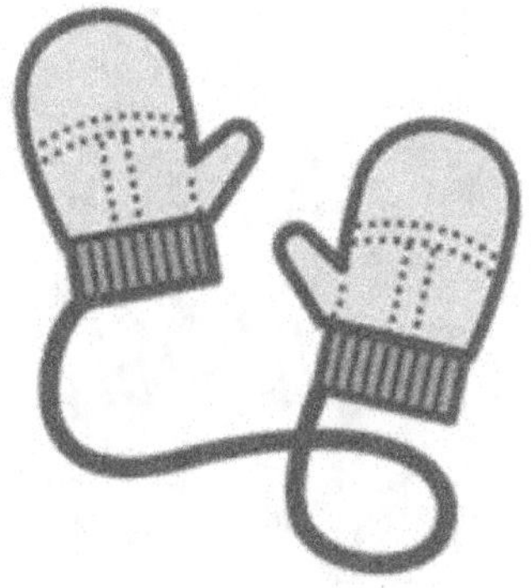

The mittens are very warm.

bonnet

beanie

The beanie is for winter.

tablier

ποδιά

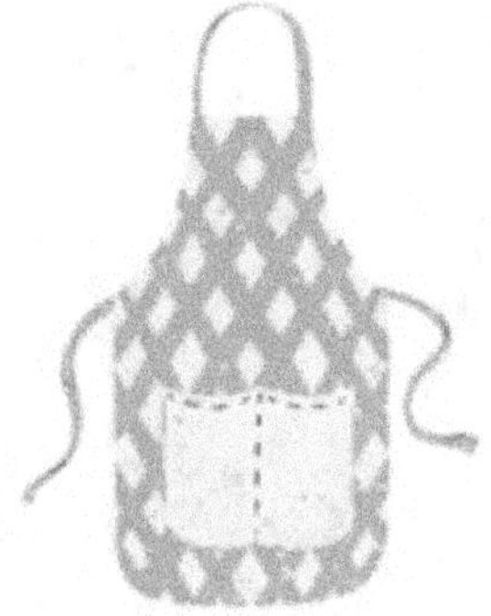

I wear my apron when I bake.

poupée

κούκλα

The doll is for my baby sister.

hochets

κουδουνίστρες

The rattle is for the baby.

jouet

παιχνίδι

The toy is very fun.

couche

πάνα

The baby has to wear a diaper.

berceau

ψάθινη κούνια

She is sleeping in her bassinet.

bavoir

σαλιάρα

My baby brother has to wear his bib when he is eating.

octogone

οκτάγωνο

The octagon is saying okay!

triangle

τρίγωνο

The triangle has three corners.

carré

τετράγωνο

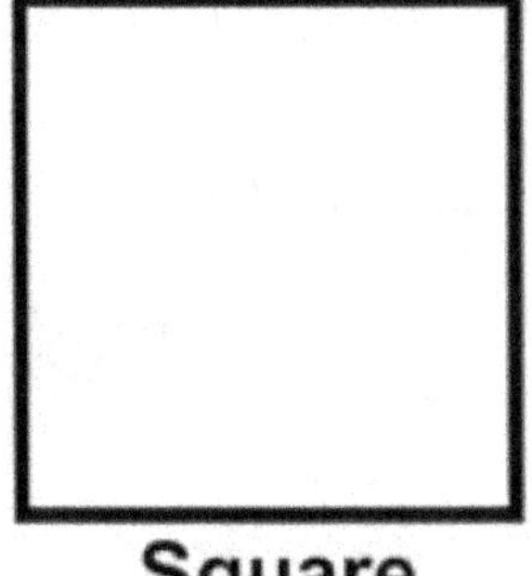

Square

The square has four sides.

cercle

κύκλος

Circle

The circle is round.

ovale

ωοειδής

The oval shape looks like a circle.

cœur

καρδιά

I drew a heart on my paper.

traverser

σταυρός

That sign is a cross.

la flèche

βέλος

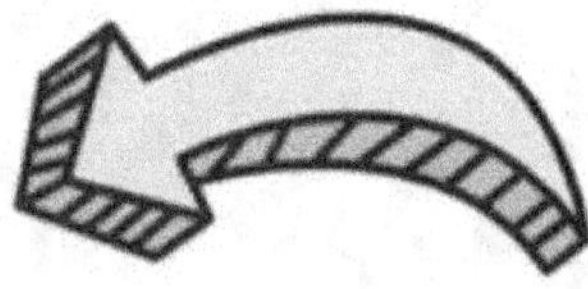

The arrow is pointing this way.

cube

κύβος

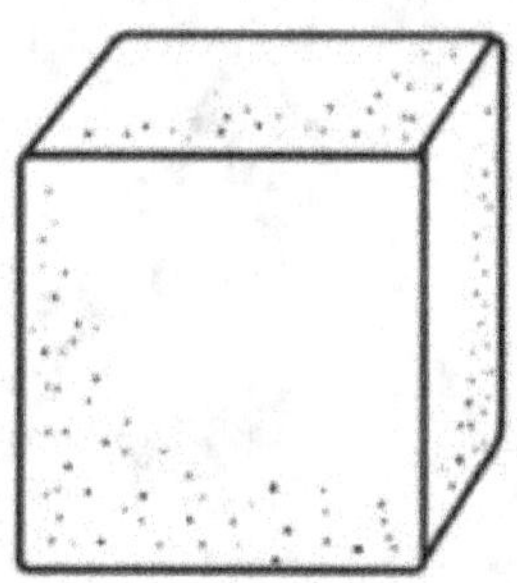

The cube is 3D.

étoile

αστέρι

The star is yellow and shiny.

tir à l'arc

τοξοβολία

The archery is where you aim.

badminton

παιγνίδι όμοιο με τέννις

My favorite sport is badminton.

criquet

κρίκετ

I am very good at cricket.

bowling

μπόουλινγκ

I got one pin down at bowling!

boxe

πυγμαχία

The boxing gloves are hot.

tennis

τένις

He can hit the ball in tennis.

faire de la planche a roulettes

σκέιτμπορντ

He skateboards to school.

planche de surf

ιστιοσανίδα

The shark loves surfing in the ocean.

le hockey

χακί

I like to play Ice hockey.

yoga

γιόγκα

He is closing his eyes and doing yoga.

épée

ξιφασκία

They are fencing and dueling together.

aptitude

κατάλληλότητα

She will do some fitness in the pool.

gymnastique

γυμναστική

He can do brilliant gymnastics.

karaté

καρατέ

She is good at kicking in Karate.

volley-ball

βόλεϊ

She is holding a volleyball.

musculation

αρση βαρών

The girl with brown hair can do weightlifting.

basketball

μπάσκετ

He can balance the ball with one finger in basketball.

base-ball

μπέιζμπολ

The little chick is in the finales at baseball.

le rugby

ράγκμπι

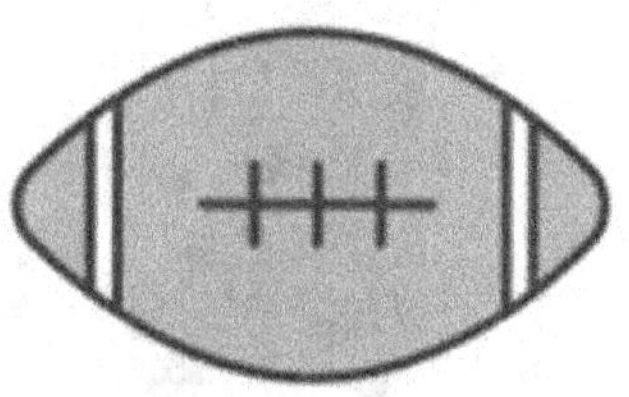

The rugby ball has white stripes.

lutte

πάλη

The sumo will compete in wrestling.

course de voitures

αγωνας αυτοκινητων

He is number one for car racing.

cyclisme

ποδηλασία

He is peacefully cycling on the road.

fonctionnement

τρέξιμο

He is running while listening to his earphones.

tennis de table

πινγκ πονγκ

My brother and dad will play table tennis.

pêche

αλιεία

He will go to the river to fish.

judo

είδος πολεμικής τέχνης

She has a red belt in Judo.

escalade

ορειβασία

He will climb the ladder.

tournage

κυνήγι

He is shooting the archery board.

le golf

γκολφ

She is going to compete in the golf competition.

balade

βόλτα

He will ride his scooter.

asseyez-vous

κάτσε κάτω

They are sitting down together.

se lever

σήκω πάνω

She likes to stand up.

bats toi

πάλη

They are fighting over the book.

rire

γέλιο

He is laughing so hard!

lis

ανάγνωση

She read a picture book.

jouer

παίζω

He went to play on the slide.

ecoutez

ακούω

He listened for the ice cream cart.

pleurer

κραυγή

He cried because he got a bad grade.

pense

νομίζω

He thought that the test would be hard.

chanter

τραγουδώ

He sang for the concert.

regarder la télévision

βλέπω τηλεόραση

He watched TV the whole night.

danse

χορός

She was a good dancer.

allumer

ανάβω

The light is turned on.

éteindre

σβήνω

The light is turned off.

gagner

νίκη

He won the contest.

mouche

πετώ

The parrot can fly.

couper

τομή

He was cutting his nails.

désinvolte

πετάω

He threw away the garbage.

dormir

υπνος

He slept soundly.

fermer

κλείσε

He closed his mouth shut.

ouvert

ανοιξε

She opened the bathroom door.

écrire

γράφω

She wrote with a pencil.

donner

δίνω

Santa gave her a present.

sauter

αλμα

She had fun jumping.

manger

τρώω

The shark ate yummy ice cream.

boisson

ποτό

The old British man drank tea.

cuisinier

μάγειρας

The microwave cooked his soup.

lavage

πλύση

You need to remember to wash your hands.

attendre

περίμενε

He was waiting for the bus.

montée

αναρρίχηση

She climbed a lot of mountains.

parler

μιλα ρε

Two best friends were talking together.

crawl

αργή πορεία

The baby crawled on the floor.

rêver

ονειρο

The Sloth dreamed about eating leaves.

creuser

σκάβω

That strong man dug a swimming pool.

taper

χειροκρότημα

The baby clapped her hands.

tricoter

πλέκω

She knits with the purple string.

coudre

ράβω

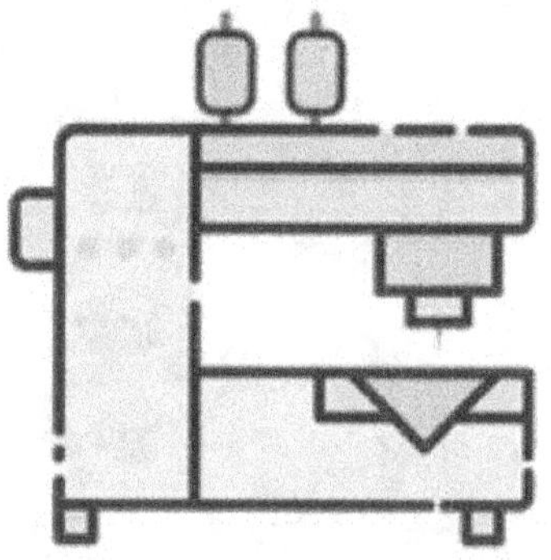

That is a sewing machine.

odeur

μυρωδιά

The perfume smelled great.

baiser

φιλί

He kissed his mother.

étreinte

αγκαλιάζω

They hugged each other.

ronfler

ροχαλίζω

The tiger snored.

baigner

λούομαι

He took a bath.

s'incliner

υποκλίσεις

He bowed to the judge.

peindre

χρώμα

He painted a colorful picture.

se plonger

κατάδυση

He dove to the deepest part of the ocean.

ski

σκι

The ski was expensive.

empiler

σωρός

The books are stacked high.

acheter

αγορά

They bought cereal.

secouer

σέικ

They shook hands together.

programmeur

προγραμματιστής

He was a smart computer programmer.

vétérinaire

κτηνίατρος

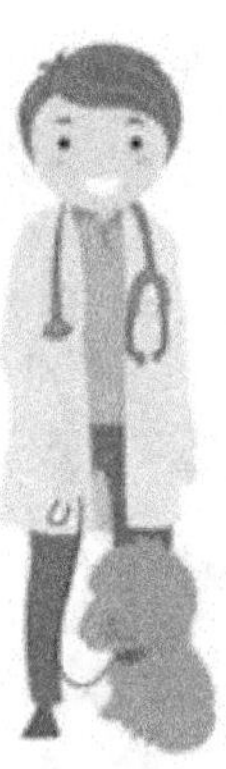

She is a veterinarian.

vendeur de rue

πλανόδιος πωλητής

That street vendor sells hot dogs.

mineur

μεταλλωρύχος

That Miner will find gold.

prof

δάσκαλος

The owl is the teacher.

groom

μπέλμπι

That Bellboy is fat.

orateur

ομιλητής

The chicken is a great Speaker.

boucher

σφάζω

The Butcher sells fish.

pharmacien

φαρμακοποιός

That Pharmacist saved a person's life.

réceptionniste

υπεύθυνος υποδοχής

He is a Receptionist.

politicien

πολιτικός

He wants to be a Politician.

guide touristique

ξεναγός

That Tour guide led us around Japan.

entrepreneur

επιχειρηματίας

He is an Entrepreneur.

danseuse de ballet

μπαλαρίνα

She is training to be a Ballet dancer.

astronaute

αστροναύτης

He is a great astronaut.

juge

δικαστής

That Judge is always fair.

avocat

δικηγόρος

The lawyer is serious.

la caissière

ταμίας

She is a cashier at the market.

conducteur de taxi

οδηγός ταξί

He is a fast Taxi driver.

plombier

υδραυλικός

That Plumber fixes toilets.

musicien

μουσικός

She wants to be a Musician like her teacher.

chef

σεφ

The chef makes fast food.

boulanger

αρτοποιός

That baker is a bread.

artiste

καλλιτέχνης

That Artist came from Italy.

acteur

ηθοποιός

That actor is famous.

barman

ποτοπώλης

The Bartender works in a bar.

coiffeur

κομμωτής

That girl is a Hairdresser.

évêques

επίσκοποι

He is a Bishop.

opticien

κατασκευαστής οπτικών ειδών

She went to an Optician.

fleuriste

ανθοπώλης

She is a great Florist.

écrivain

συγγραφέας

He is a famous author.

comptable

λογιστής

My accountant is loyal.

du vin

κρασί

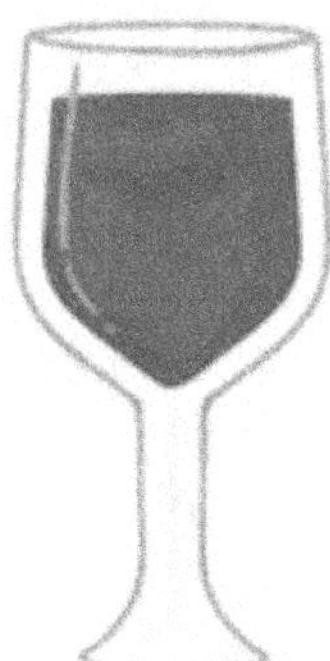

That wine tastes good.

café

καφές

That coffee is bitter.

limonade

λεμονάδα

The lemonade is refreshing.

chocolat chaud

ζεστή σοκολάτα

I drink hot chocolate every day.

milk-shake

milkshake

The milkshake has whipped cream.

eau

νερό

The water is not cold.

thé

τσάι

The tea is hot.

lait

γάλα

Milk is white.

bière

μπύρα

The beer is foamy.

un soda

σόδα

The soda is fizzy.

smoothie

smoothie

The smoothie is a watermelon flavor.

milk-shake

milkshake

The milkshake has whipped cream.

lait de coco

γάλα καρύδας

The coconut milk is yummy.

du jus d'orange

χυμός πορτοκάλι

The orange juice is made from oranges.

cacao

κακάο

The cocoa is sweet.

fromage

τυρί

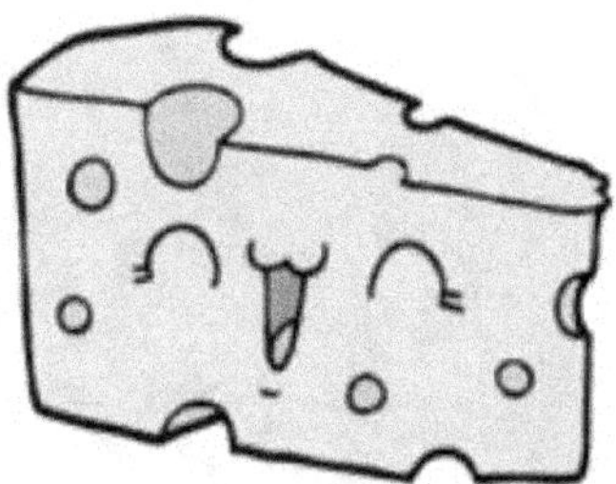

The cheese is creamy.

oeuf

αυγό

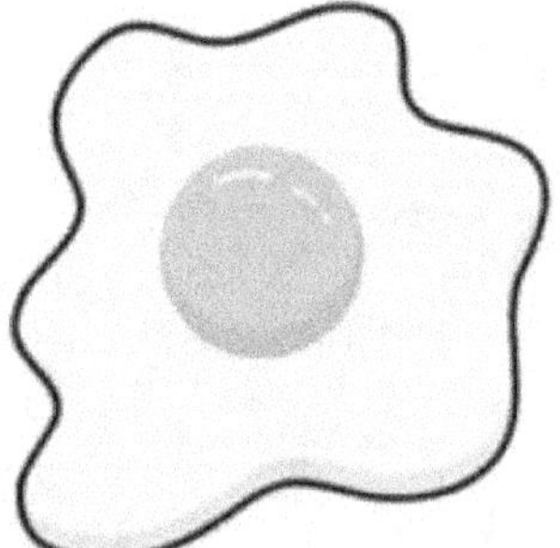

The egg is fried.

beurre

βούτυρο

The butter is put on bread.

margarine

μαργαρίνη

Margarine looks like butter.

yaourt

γιαούρτι

That yogurt is popular.

cottage cheese

τυρί cottage

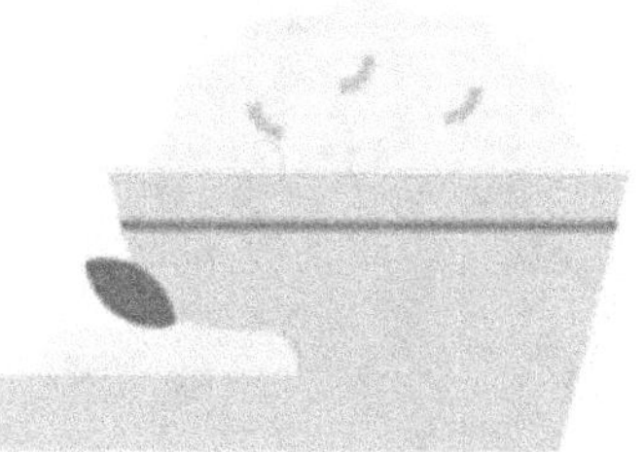

The cottage cheese is put on crackers.

crème glacée

παγωτό

They have a triple scoop ice cream.

crème

κρέμα

That is a lot of creams.

sandwich

σάντουιτς

That sandwich is healthy.

saucisse

λουκάνικο

Americans love sausages.

hamburger

χάμπουργκερ

That hamburger looks happy.

hot-dog

λουκάνικο

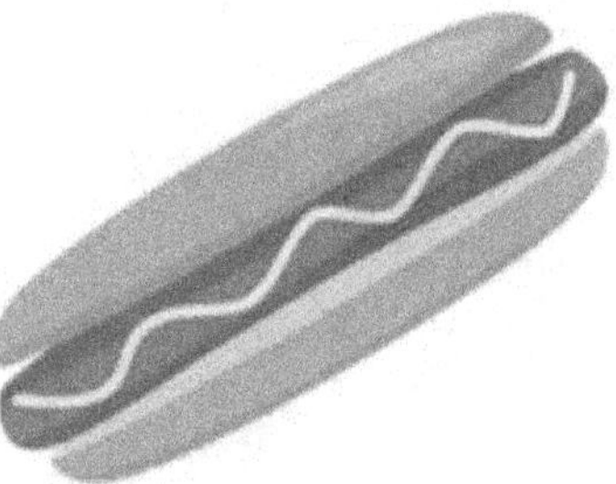

That hot dog has mustard on it.

pain

ψωμί

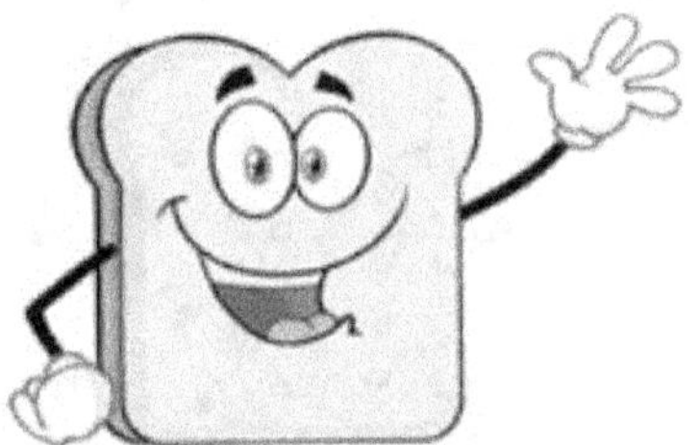

That bread is saying hello.

pizza

πίτσα

That pizza is cheesy.

steak

μπριζόλα

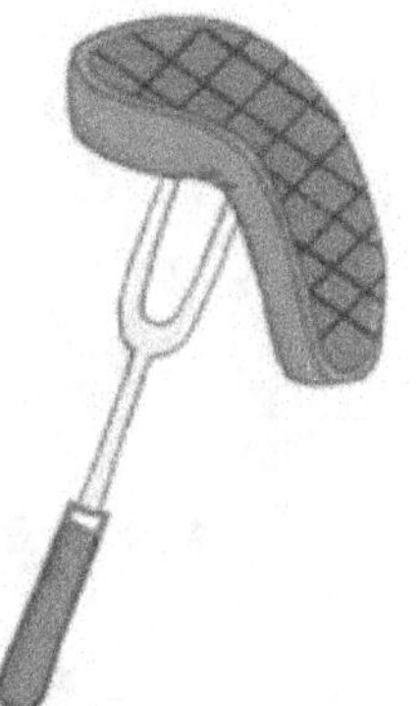

The steak was grilled.

poulet rôti

ψητό κοτόπουλο

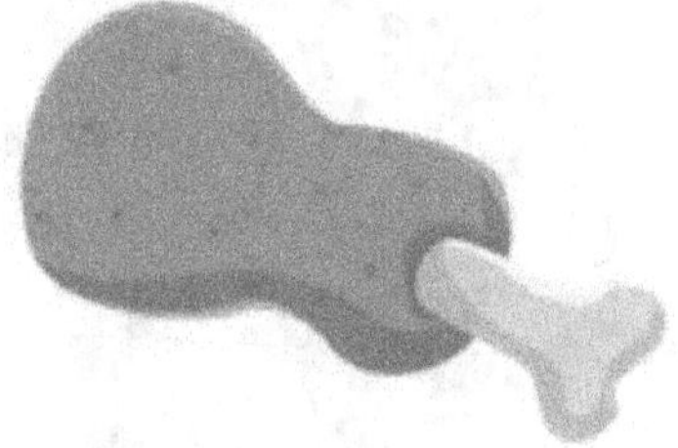

Roast Chicken is delicious.

poisson

ψάρι

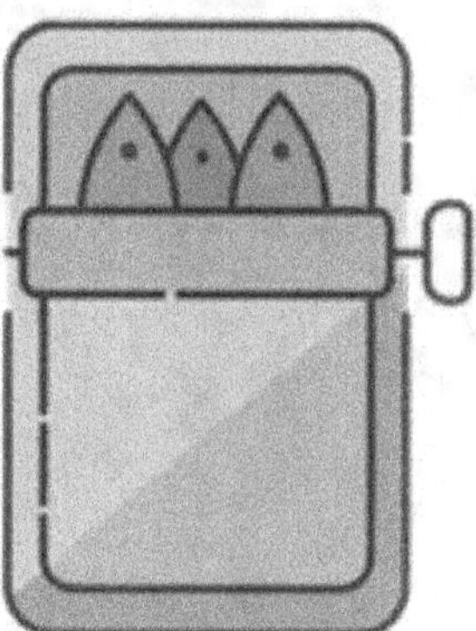

You can buy canned fish in the market.

fruit de mer

θαλασσινά

Lobster is expensive seafood.

jambon

ζαμπόν

Ham can be put in sandwiches.

kebab

κεμπάπ

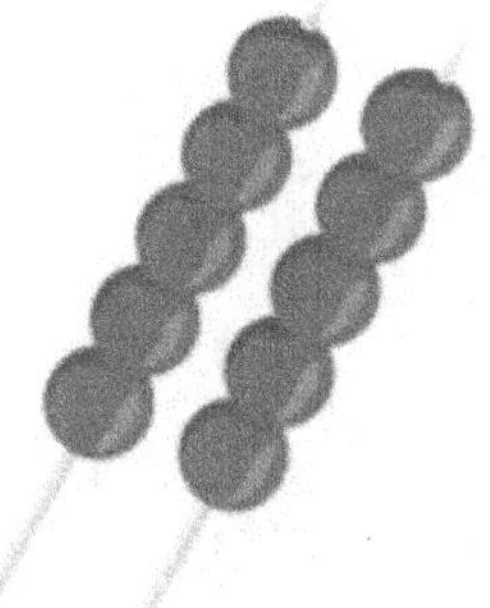

Kebab is a delicacy in America.

bacon

μπέικον

That bacon is smiling.

crème fraîche

κρέμα γάλακτος

You can dip your chips in sour cream.

vache

αγελάδα

Cows are black and white.

lapin

κουνέλι

That rabbit is fun to play with.

canard

πάπια

That duck is content.

crevette

γαρίδα

The shrimp has six legs.

porc

χοίρος

That pig is pink and fat.

abeille

μέλισσα

The bee has a stinger.

chèvre

γίδα

That goat has a white horn.

crabe

κάβουρας

The crab has two big pincers.

cerf

ελάφι

That deer is sleeping.

dinde

τουρκία

The turkey has a giant tail.

colombe

περιστέρι

That dove is carrying a plant.

mouton

πρόβατο

That sheep has fluffy wool.

poisson

ψάρι

That fish has colorful fins.

poulet

κοτόπουλο

That chicken is waking everybody up.

cheval

αλογο

The horse has a red mane.

chaise

καρέκλα

That wing chair is yellow.

meuble tv

βάση τηλεόρασης

The TV stand can hold books.

canapé

καναπές

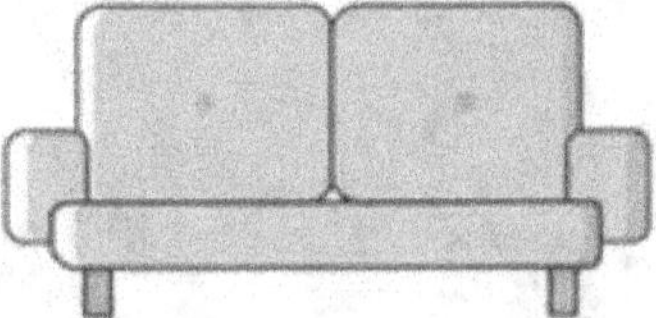

The sofa is comfortable to sit on.

coussins

μαξιλάρια

The cushion helps soften your seat.

téléphone

τηλέφωνο

The telephone is ringing.

télévision

τηλεόραση

That television is big.

haut-parleurs

ηχεία

That speaker is used to increase the volume.

table d'appoint

πλαϊνό τραπέζι

That end table is sparkling clean.

service à thé

σετ τσαγιου

That tea set is from China.

cheminée

τζάκι

The fireplace makes me warm.

télécommandes

τηλεχειριστήρια

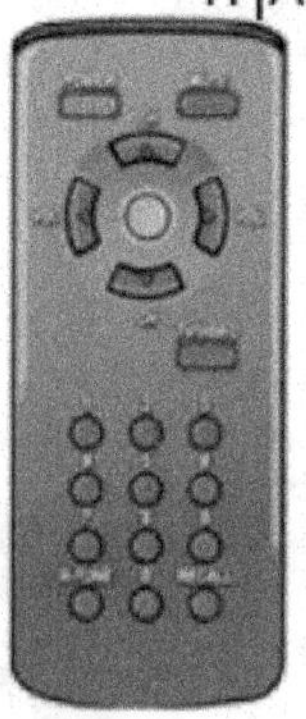

The remote has lots of buttons.

ventilateur électrique

ανεμιστήρας

The fan is blowing wind.

lampadaire

λαμπα πατωματος

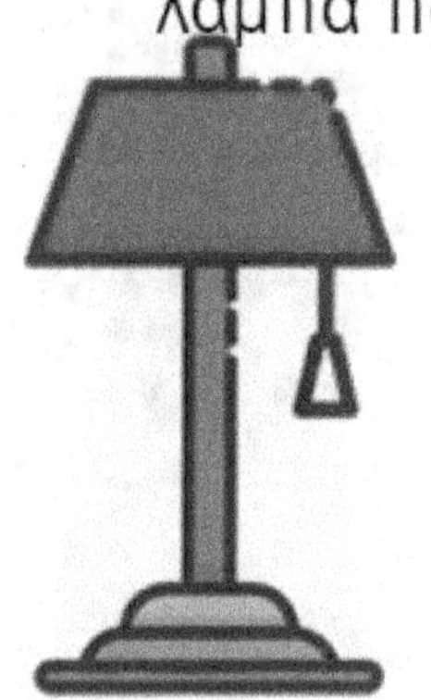

The floor lamp is very tall.

tapis

χαλί

The carpet is soft and silky.

bureaux

γραφεία

The table is made of wood.

stores

τυφλοί

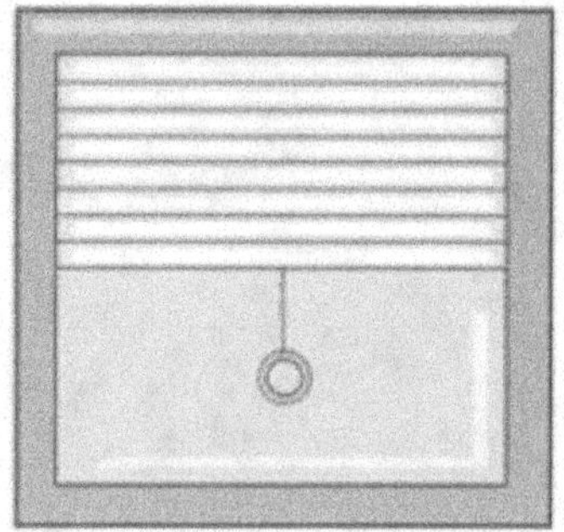

I will pull the blinds down.

rideaux

κουρτίνες

She opened the curtains.

image

εικόνα

The picture is about the mountains and the sky.

vase

βάζο

The roses are all in a vase.

l'horloge

ρολόι

The alarm clock is beeping.

oreiller

μαξιλάρι

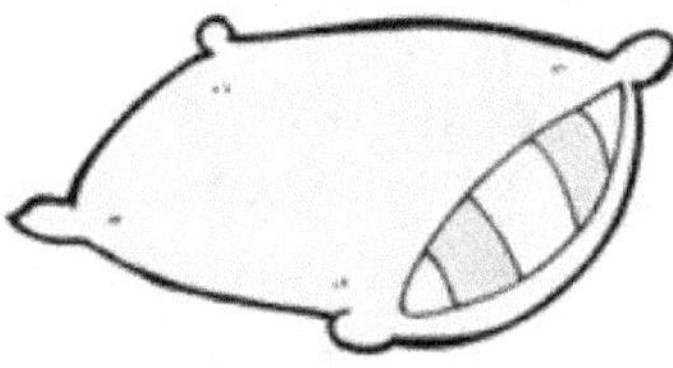

The pillow is pink and yellow.

cintre

κρεμάστρα καπέλων

The hat stand has only one hat on it.

mettre la table

μπουντουάρ

I have made up on my dressing table.

lampe de table

επιτραπέζιο φωτιστικό

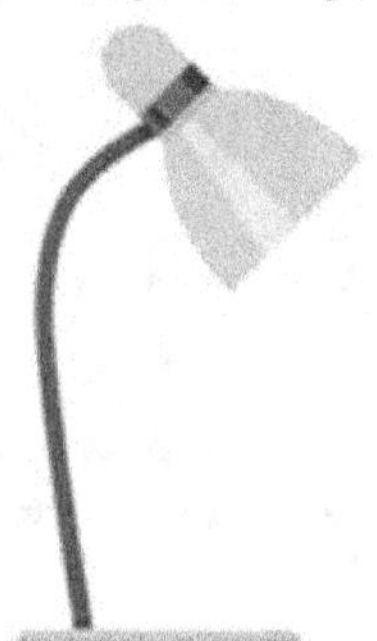

The table lamp will help me see in the dark.

miroir

καθρέφτης

The mirror is very tall.

planche a repasser

σιδερώστρα

Don't touch the ironing board, it's hot!

boîte avec tiroir

κουτί με συρτάρι

You can keep your clothes in the hope chest.

table de chevet

κομοδίνο

The nightstand has my lamp on it.

lit

κρεβάτι

The bed is charming.

climatisation

κλιματιστικό

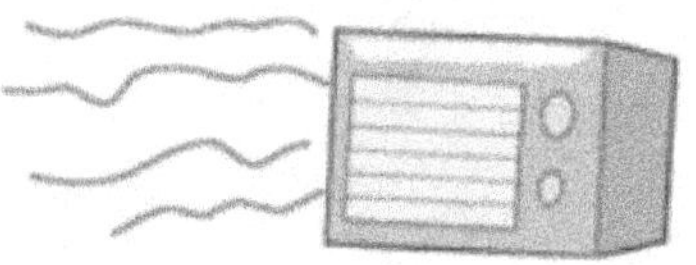

The air conditioner is cold.

cruche

κανάτα

The measuring jug has nothing inside.

dentifrice

οδοντόκρεμα

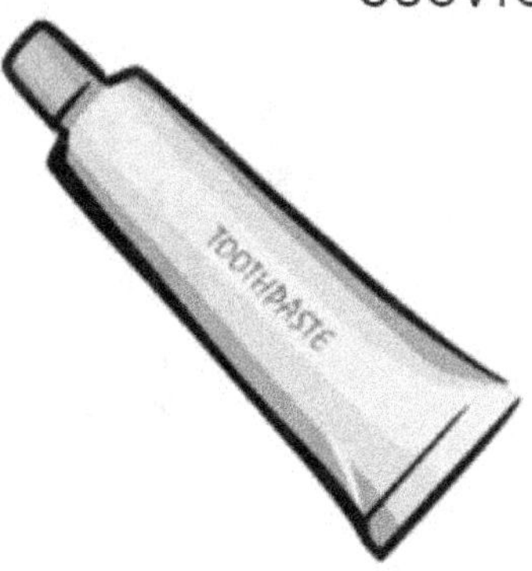

The toothpaste is mint flavored.

brosse à dents

οδοντόβουρτσα

The toothbrush has toothpaste on it.

savon

σαπούνι

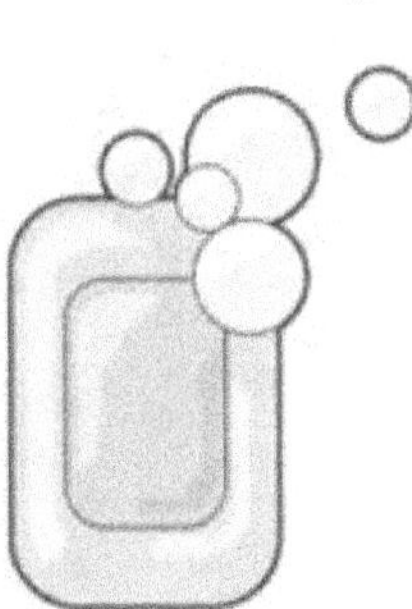

The soap is very bubbly.

pince à linge

μανταλάκι

The clothespin will clip my clothes.

cintre

κρεμάστρα

The hanger is hanging my boots.

sèche-cheveux

στεγνωτήρας μαλλιών

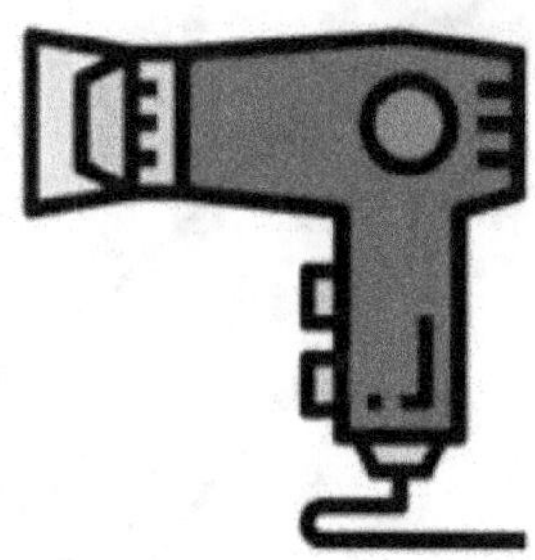

The hairdryer will blow my hair.

shampooing

σαμπουάν

The shampoo is used to clean your hair.

bulle

φυσαλλίδα

The bubbles are very fun to play in.

brosse

βούρτσα

She is brushing her hair with the brush.

papier toilette

χαρτί υγείας

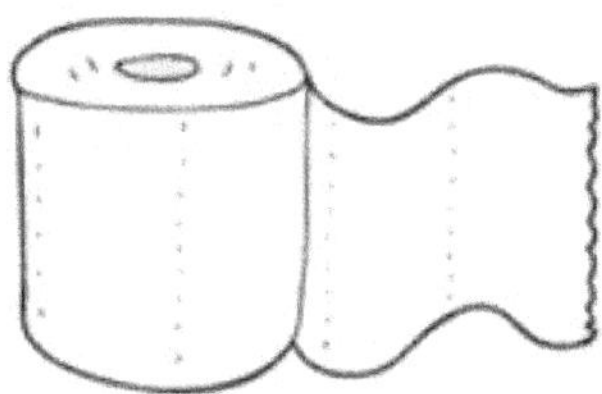

The toilet paper is used to dry your hands.

serviette

πετσέτα

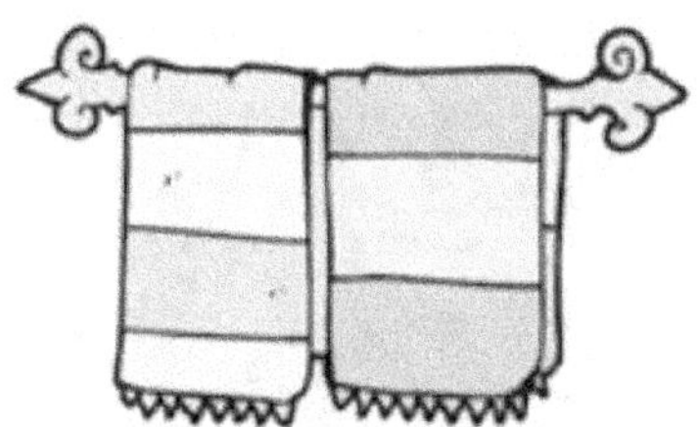

We have two towels on the rack.

corde à linge

άπλωμα

My shirt is hanging on the clothesline.

douche

ντους

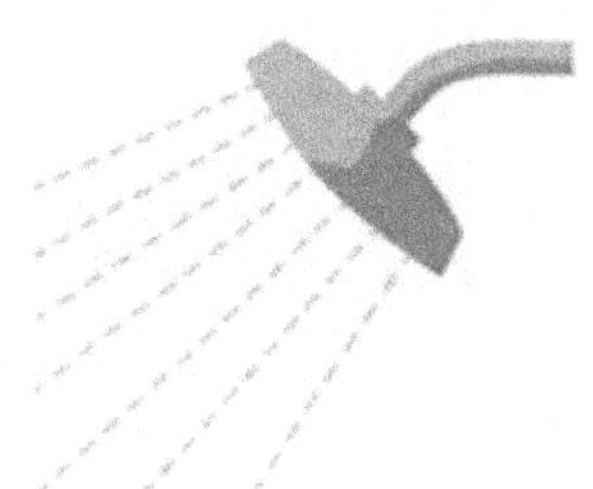

The shower is spraying water.

baignoire

μπανιέρα

The bathtub is comfortable.

lessive

απορρυπαντικό πλυντηρίου

The laundry detergent is used with the washing machine.

seau

κάδος

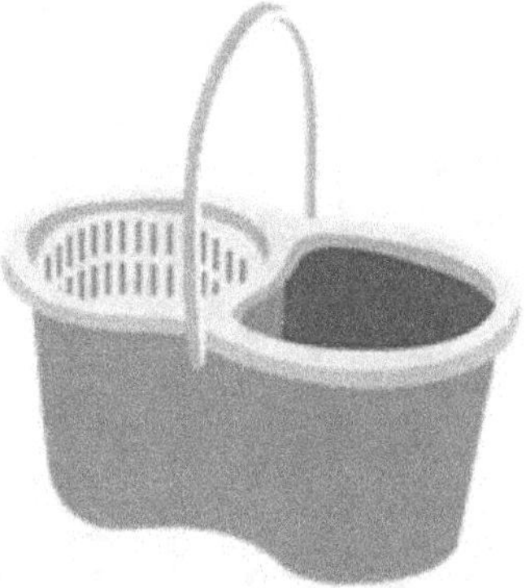

Can you help me fill up the bucket?

vadrouilles

σφουγγαρίστρες

The mop is used for mopping the floor.

savon liquide

υγρό σαπούνι

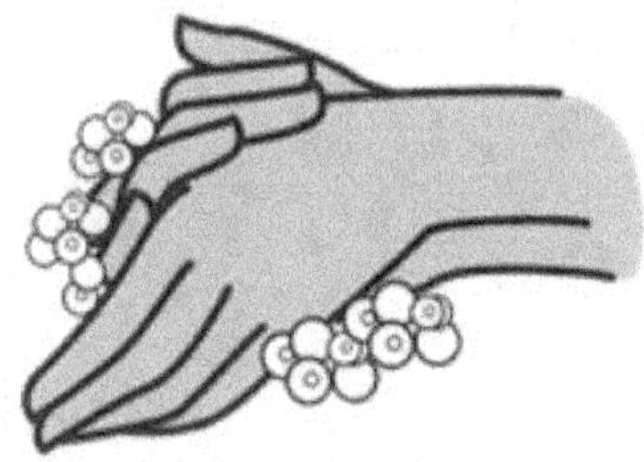

I use soapy water to wash my hands.

lessive en poudre

σκόνη πλυσίματος

I will scoop up the washing powder.

sac poubelle

σακούλα σκουπιδιών

The trash bag is full of trash.

poubelle

σκουπιδοτενεκές

You have only to put recylcle trash in the trash can.

les puits

νεροχύτες

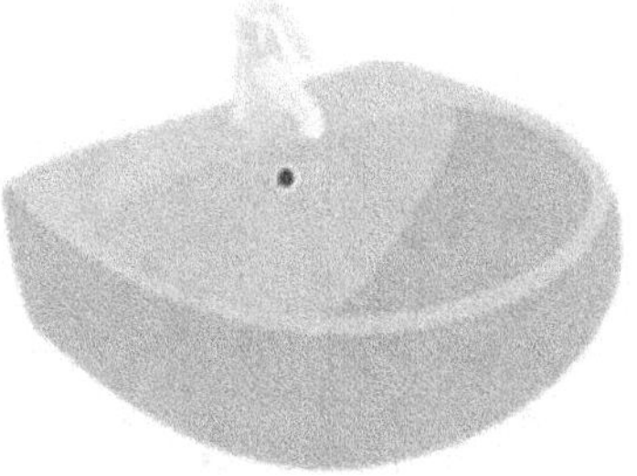

You should wash your hands in the sink.

cuvette des toilettes

λεκανη τουαλετας

She let her bunny use the toilet.

machine à laver

πλυντήριο

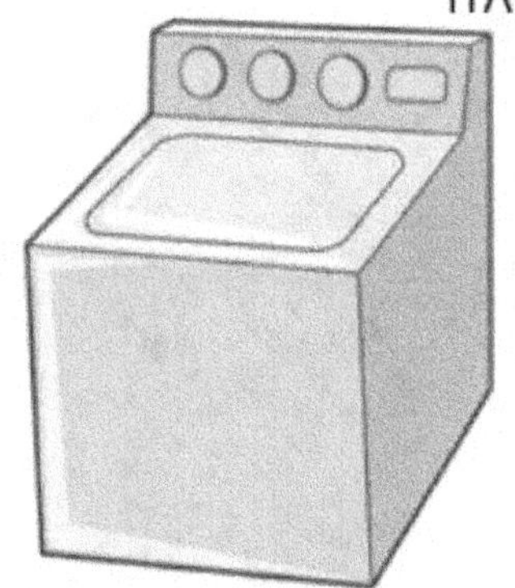

The washing machine wash your clothes.

panier à linge

καλάθι άπλυτων

She is putting all the clothes into the laundry basket.

le rasoir

ξυράφι

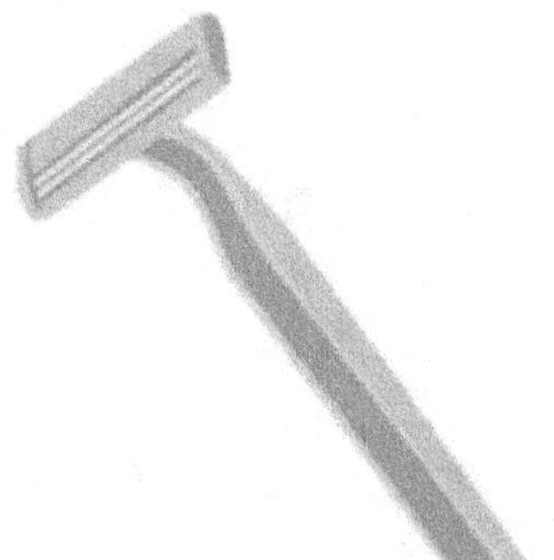

He uses the razor to shave his beard.

rasoir électrique

ηλεκτρικό ξυράφι

The electric razor works faster than the normal one.

crème à raser

κρέμα ξυρίσματος

The shaving cream is fluffy.

bain de bouche

στοματικό διάλυμα

The mouthwash smells very lovely.

coton-tige

βαμβάκι

Q-tip can be used for many things.

brosse à cheveux

βούρτσα μαλλιών

She brushes her hair with her hairbrush.

peigne

χτένα

Her dad will comb her hair for her.

nettoyant

καθαριστικό

Put the cap back on the cleanser bottle.

échelle

κλίμακα

You can measure things on the scale.

papier de soie

χαρτομάντηλο

The tissue is on the counter.

jouets de bain

παιχνίδια μπάνιου

The little duck is a bath toy.

robinet

βρύση

The faucet is broken.

miroir

καθρέφτης

He is looking in the mirror.

tapis de bain

χαλί μπάνιου

The bath mat is purple and yellow.